with best wishes

Noel Blackburn

ONE MAN AND HIS DOG GO WALKIES:

John o'Groats to Land's End.

Noel Blackham

By the same author -

IT'S A SMALL WORLD - a musical play
LE MONDE EST UNE CHANSON - a collection of French poems
IT'S A DOG'S LIFE - the story of Birmingham Dogs' Home

ONE MAN AND HIS DOG GO WALKIES:
JOHN O'GROATS TO LAND'S END

Noel Blackham

With illustrations by the author

First published 1991, by WORLD MUSICALS,
28 Wilsford Green, Edgbaston, BIRMINGHAM B15 3UG

Second impression 1993

ISBN 0 9517303 0 4

Printed in the UK by Husband & Currell, Ltd,
240 Holliday Street, Birmingham B1 1SJ
Bound by J W Braithwaite & Son, Ltd,
Pountney Street, Wolverhampton WV2 4HY

ONE MAN AND HIS DOG GO WALKIES: John o'Groats to Land's End

NOEL BLACKHAM

This is the true story of how one man and his dog walked from JOHN
O'GROATS to LAND'S END. The walk began on Wednesday 13th April 1988,
and ended on Tuesday 24th May, taking 41 days, 5 hours and 55 minutes.

NOTE. The author describes the route in great detail, and refers to the
numbers of the roads and the mileage, so that the reader may go over the
precise route, with the aid of maps.

It is pointed out that the sections containing the thirty-inch-wide
hard shoulder are not very suitable for walking, and that an alternative
route might be preferred. This applies particularly to that part of the
A74 trunk road between Lesmahagow and Lockerbie.

ONE MAN AND HIS DOG GO WALKIES:

John o'Groats to Land's End

PART TWO.

1. HOW IT ALL STARTED.

Mary suddenly remarked:

"I'd love to walk from John o'Groats to Land's End."

She could not have realised it, but in pronouncing those few words, she had sown the seeds of an idea which was to grow and grow.

Roy Hayward, Sid and Mary Francis and I, not forgetting Monique, my cross-collie, were enjoying one of our cosy little rambles in the depths of the Wyre Forest, near Kidderminster.

"I've tried it - twice," said I, "1969 and 1973."

"What happened?"

"Didn't get out of Scotland! 1969, got as far as Bridge of Orchy - 247 miles in ten days. Poor water-proofing - split open. Soaked with rain, three or four days running!"

"And 1973?"

"Worse! 186 miles in eight days, as far as Spean Bridge. Blisters were the problem, this time."

Yes, already twice in my lifetime, during the summer months of 1969 and 1973, I had gaily set off from John o'Groats, and it is quite likely that, if Mary had not made that casual remark, the possibility of making a third attempt would never have occurred to me.

Thank you, Mary.

2. THE IDEA GROWS.

The idea, which had lain dormant all those years, was now awakened, and I began to consider the possibility of having another go. At first, it was just a crazy idea - no more than wishful thinking, but the more I thought about the practical problems involved, the more it seemed like a feasible proposition. One thing was sure from the start - my six-year-old cross-collie, Monique, who, in 1983, had spent part of her life as a resident of the Birmingham Dogs' Home, would have to come with me.

Once more, I felt the inspiration and motivation which had prompted my earlier efforts of 1969 and 1973. Since I was now retired, I had the freedom to use my time as I wished. I could, therefore, give a lot more attention to the project, and make a more determined attempt to complete the full distance, end to end.

It was not an idea to be toyed with! The project would require all my attention, and would have to take priority over all others. It was a personal challenge, to be taken by the horns, a test of endurance and an exciting adventure. There was a certain fascination in walking from end to end of one's native island. The very names, John o'Groats and Land's End had a ring about them - almost an aura of mystery!

There would be two golden rules. Firstly, the whole journey had to be done on foot, using only the physical capabilities of the human frame - or, in Monique's case, the canine frame. Secondly, there was to be no back-up team to deal with such matters as accommodation, route, feeding, first aid and other emergencies.

On our next ramble, Roy, Monique and I were visiting Leamington Spa and the site of a Saxon mill, at nearby Guy's Cliffe. Crossing a field, I confided in Roy my thoughts about walking from John o'Groats to Land's End. Somewhat to my surprise, he thought it was an idea worth pursuing, and not at all unthinkable.

With steadily mounting excitement, I began to mention my project to friends and acquaintances. Then it occurred to me that the more I spoke about the walk, the more the onus would be on me to change my words into deeds. If I were not already committed, I soon should be!

I was sometimes asked why I was doing it. Some thought the attempt ought to be widely publicised, and that I should seek sponsorship. Some people thought I must be mad. At least two asked:

"Do you think you are wise?"

Well, there was no answer to that, because, being realistic, I knew there was some truth in what was implied. The fact was, that I could by no means feel confident of achieving my goal. How could I be certain of surviving more than three or four days of continuous walking, when I had already failed twice, when 15 years younger, and presumably fitter? Not only that, I was now on two hospital waiting lists for minor operations, so it could not be said that I was in the ideal condition to tackle such an event as this.

I did not fancy the idea of publicising the attempt, only for it to fail ignominiously!

On the question of raising money for charity, I find it strange for people to donate money, just because some exploit or feat of strength is being attempted. Of course, it is good that they are encouraged to give generously to worthy causes, and similarly, it is good when a person can enjoy the thrill of meeting a challenge that he has set himself, but the logical connection between the two eludes me.

However uncertain the outcome of the project seemed, once I had the bit between my teeth, even wild horses could not have induced me to turn from my chosen course. Just to ensure that I should not come up against the disapproval and displeasure of the medical profession, I decided not to inform the hospital, or my doctor, about the walk, until preparations were well under way. With a little luck, the hospital would not require me at an inconvenient time.

3. MAKING PLANS.

Examining the route that I had taken previously, I considered it to be as good as any. It would obviously be an advantage to use roads with which I was already partly familiar. In fact, part of my route had been considerably shortened since my last effort. A bridge had been built at North Ballachulish, which crossed the narrow strip of water between Loch Linnhe and Loch Leven. This would make it unnecessary to go all the way round Loch Leven, and so reduce the journey by about 12 miles, assuming, of course, that the bridge catered for pedestrians, as well as vehicles.

The route through Glasgow would have to be well worked out, using a street plan, while the densely populated areas of South Lancashire would also call for careful map-reading.

When I came to Cheshire, I looked at two routes, one via Tarporley, and one via Sandbach. It was not until a day or two before leaving home that I decided on the latter. There were three advantages - the country was more familiar, there were good footpaths, and the distance was about two miles shorter!

At least, I should have no difficulty in finding the way through my home town, the city of Birmingham. In fact, I should make it one of the overnight stops, and so be able to put my feet up at home for one night!

Bristol, the other large city to be negotiated, seemed to have more problems than Glasgow, but again, with the aid of a street plan, the way through became clear. Indeed, the most direct route passed just west of the city centre.

The section between Tiverton and Okehampton, in Devon, was a matter of opinion, but, apart from that, the rest of the route was obvious.

I estimated that we could average 25 miles a day. At that rate, we should complete the total distance of 873 miles in 35 days.

Spring, no doubt, would be the ideal time of year for walking. The temperatures would be quite tolerable, and the days would be long enough to do the mileage. It was not my intention to walk after dark. Spring, 1988, was six months away, so we should have time to get organised, book accommodation, and get into training.

A dental appointment, on the 7th April, was the factor to determine our date of departure for the far north. So as to avoid travelling over the busy weekend, I delayed our start until Monday evening, 11th April.

I was now able to fix the precise dates of all the overnight stops, so I wrote to the various regional tourist boards for information. Lots of attractive and colourful brochures soon began to arrive in the post.

The next item on the agenda was to decide just where to finish each stage. It was not possible, of course, to make stops at exactly 25-mile intervals. Some stages would have to be longer, some shorter. Once the stopping points were fixed, I could then sit down and choose the precise accommodation for each stop - quite a pleasant occupation for the winter evenings.

Before long, we had somewhere to stay for most of the stages across Scotland, and later on, as far as the Midlands. Was I becoming somewhat optimistic in booking so far along the route, I wondered, but experience had taught me how important it was to have accommodation waiting, at the end of a day's walking.

Strangely enough, I had difficulty in finding somewhere to stay, at Wick, our first 'port of call', but, with the help of the very efficient local tourist information centre, I eventually arranged to stay with the very same lady I had stayed with in 1973!

The two things I looked for, when choosing accommodation, after the cost, were the matter of diet, and the acceptance of pets. As I did not eat game, poultry or sea-food, I decided to simplify matters and ask for a vegetarian evening meal. I might as well go the whole hog - or should I say 'forgo' the whole hog?

As for pets, they were accepted at about half the bed and breakfast establishments, hotels, guest houses and farms.

Meanwhile, I bought some of the various pieces of equipment, that I should need on the 'grand tour' - maps, a suitable ruck-sack, a reliable water-proof, and a splendid collection of socks!

During our training walks, I discovered which parts of my feet were most vulnerable, but usually, the fault could be traced to the footwear. I experimented with a very light pair of running shoes, but these always produced a blister - and in the same spot!

I then tried walking shoes (some might prefer boots) with commando-type soles and heels. Though fairly heavy, the deep tread and the thick soles would lessen some of the impact of foot meeting ground, as well as minimising the effect of uneven ground and stone chippings.

It is worth while paying some attention to the materials of which a shoe is made. The parts of the shoe that have to take most of the wear, through contact with the ground, should, preferably, be of a heavy-duty, synthetic material, while the parts surrounding the foot would be better made of leather, rather than rubber or latex, to give the foot air.

This was the type of shoe I chose.

4. ON THE FITNESS TRAIL.

There was not much point in embarking on an exercise on this scale, without first of all going through a sort of toughening up programme, to get the body in tune to meet the severe physical demands, that were soon to be made of it.

In November, Monique and I began to increase our daily mileage from two to two and a half miles, then to three, three and a half, and so on. In so doing, we were able to discover new territory, which added greatly to the interest and variety of our walks. Sometimes, we walked into the centre of Birmingham, sometimes along a canal, sometimes along a disused railway line, round a reservoir, or through a country park. At the same time, we kept up our rambles of six to eight miles.

It was on one of these rambles, on the 22nd January, 1988, that Ken Westley, a founder member of the Midland Veterans' Athletic Club, led us over Kinver Edge. This was not quite as disastrous as it sounds, Kinver Edge being a popular beauty spot, lying near the border of Staffordshire and Worcestershire.

The fact that the ground was covered with a fresh fall of snow gave the ramble a certain spice. Bearing in mind the vagaries of the British climate, who could say we should not encounter snow, at some time during our ramble through Scotland and England? At least, we were now prepared for such an eventuality - as well as the occasional tumble!

As well as training for fitness, Monique also had to master the art of travelling by train. She made her début on British Rail on Saturday, 20th February, when we travelled from Birmingham University to Redditch, changing trains at King's Norton, en route.

With great excitement, Monique boarded her first train, and took to this new mode of travel like a duck to water! Why were all those people sitting in her carriage with, apparently, nothing much to do? She would go and say hello to everyone within range, being a very sociable dog, by nature. There were none whose frigidity did not melt a little, faced by such infectious bonhomie!

The following week, we made a trip to Kidderminster, and walked the sixteen miles back to Edgbaston. This gave us an opportunity to call on our friends, Ken and Maisie, during our walk.

Ken pointed out that I should be walking from John o'Groats because I wanted to, and knew what it involved, while Monique was doing the walk by chance, whether she wanted to, or not.

On the other hand, dogs are such staunch companions that, given the choice, they will stick with their master or mistress, through thick and thin, rather than be left behind, not quite sure whether their owner has deserted them, or if he or she will return one day, and if so, when.

Monique's passion for British Rail increased with each journey that followed. We gradually extended the range of these journeys, travelling out by train, and then returning home on foot. On the longer distances, our average speed was about three and three-quarter miles per hour.

Like most dogs, Monique is very observant, and knows when something is afoot. What is more, she likes to be in the action! Every time that I prepared to go out, she would take note, with mounting excitement, and unlike most females, she would always be the first to be ready to leave!

These early walks served not only to increase our stamina, but also to toughen up our feet. However, whereas I could change shoes and socks as required, Monique relied solely on the paws given to her by nature!

Following a long walk, she would sometimes show a little discomfort when putting her left hind paw to the ground. Fortunately, the soreness soon disappeared, but it was a matter which gave some concern, and could not be treated lightly. It was one of the problems to emerge from these preparatory outings, which were serving as trial runs.

A friend once suggested that Monique could wear bootees, similar to those worn by babies. I never tried out the idea, so I am not sure what Monique's reaction would have been, or whether bootees would have lasted many miles ... some made of leather, perhaps?

By March, we were doing at least five miles every day, and learning - from experience! On one of our walks, from Droitwich to Edgbaston, we stumbled upon the Bromsgrove By-pass, and discovered what an uninspiring stretch of road, it was. I decided that, next time, we would go through the town centre.

On Saturday 12th March, we walked from Bromsgrove to Worcester, and back - a distance of about 23 miles. On these last two outings, as well as increasing our distance, we had also sampled the route we should take when we did the actual walk ... assuming we got that far!

We examined another section of our proposed route, on Thursday 17th March, when we walked from Stone to Newcastle (Staffordshire), and back, 18 miles. We were impressed by the excellent footpaths, and we made two other interesting discoveries. Firstly, somewhere on our route, we were bound to come across road-works, and these might, or might not, obstruct our progress. Secondly, when you use a subway to cross a busy junction, you may find yourself surfacing some way off, but still on the same side of the road you were on, before you went down into the underworld. This was all good experience!

A few days later, we went straight through the centre of Birmingham and out to Minworth. For a change of scenery, we used canal towpaths on the return journey, making a total distance of 19 miles.

Our next walk was a 24-mile circular tour of the Black Country, and the last part of it, from Coseley to Edgbaston, followed the line of our proposed route from John o'Groats.

Just off the road, by Swan Village, was a shady pool, where Monique was able to indulge in one of her favourite pastimes, jumping into water and splashing around, especially on a hot day. She is not too concerned about the cleanliness of the water - any muddy puddle will do! She came out of this particular water reasonably clean, and much refreshed. When next we passed this way, the facility would again provide Monique with a moment of ecstasy - we could be sure of that!

The time to set off for bonny Scotland was fast approaching, so, on Good Friday, 1st April, we embarked on our toughest test so far - a walk from Stratford-upon-Avon to Edgbaston.

Unfortunately, the map I was using was not quite up to date. Since its publication, someone had, rather inconsiderately, decided to build a motorway, which completely blocked off our road. As a result, we had to make an unscheduled detour! Our journey was thus increased to 26 miles,

and took eight hours. Still, in retrospect, the experience was probably
good preparation for the events which lay ahead.

For all our training, we still had not walked more than 20 miles on
consecutive days. This was a novelty we should be savouring before very
long!

Richard Watts, the 'vet', gave Monique an examination, and she came
through her 'medical' with flying colours! I was not so convinced about
my own fitness, but my doctor prescribed just the right treatment. Both
Monique and I had our supply of vitamin and mineral tablets.

It was time to make the final preparations, purchase train-tickets,
and pack the ruck-sack. I thought it was too well packed, when I picked
it up, but there did not seem to be anything else that I could cross off
the list.

Three days later, we ventured forth into the unknown! Well, it was
for Monique, at least!

5. OFF WE GO!

My good friend, Will, had kindly offered to drive us to the station
in his car, so, on Monday evening, 11th April, we set off for New Street
Station, as planned. Roy also came along, to complete the farewells.

It was not long before we met with our first mishap. While waiting
on the platform, I suddenly discovered that my wrist-watch was no longer
on my wrist. Then I remembered something falling by my feet, during the
car journey. At the time, I had assumed it to be Monique's lead, but it
now seemed more likely to have been my watch.

It was too late to go back and check, but to be without a timepiece
while walking all the way from John o'Groats, would be both inconvenient
and irritating. Roy immediately came to the rescue, by offering to lend
me his watch. In the meantime, he would use my watch, which he would be
able to pick up, on returning to the car.

The train, due to depart at 22.10, was first reported to be running
'on time', but, quite suddenly, it appeared to have met with some delay.
The delay became greater. After half an hour, we were still waiting for
news of the train.

The longer we waited, the colder it became, and I was concerned for
Will and Roy, who were not suitably kitted out for a long wait on a cold

and draughty platform. They both bravely insisted on seeing it through, however, and eventually, the reluctant train pulled in.

Monique and I quietly climbed on board, Will and Roy wished us 'bon voyage', and we were left to reflect on the adventure that lay ahead.

It transpired that a broken rail had been responsible for the hold-up. On its approach to the station, the train had had to make a detour. However, it made little difference to us, since we had about an hour and a half to make our connection at Crewe, at 00.45, on Tuesday.

I looked at Monique. This was easily the longest train journey she had made, and the first time she had travelled all through the night. I wondered how she felt.

Rather like a child, slightly uneasy at first, she marvelled at the new sensations - the vibrations of the carriage, the strange noises, the movement into the darkness, and the occasional brilliant lights, seeming to flash past the windows. Perhaps she was feeling a bit like Professor Neil Armstrong, when he blasted off into space, on his way to the moon!

After all our previous train journeys, we had walked back home, the same day. Could it be that Monique was contemplating a return from John o'Groats - all in one go?

Dawn was breaking as the train pulled out of Perth, at around 5.30. Through the carriage window, I could see that the hills had a thin layer of snow. When we reached Dalwhinnie, in the Highlands, snowflakes could be seen, falling gently, like tiny parachutes.

As the daylight slowly increased, magnificent mountain scenery with streams and snow-filled crevasses emerged from the darkness. It was not long before we spotted our first sheep. From now on, these animals were sure to follow us, wherever we went!

A little further north, near the Cairngorms, snow was falling thick and fast! Oh dear, what had I let us in for?

"Do you think you are wise?", echoed a voice from the past.

At 9.00 a.m., we were in Inverness. As we now had around two and a half hours to spare, before the departure of the train for Wick, we took the opportunity to go out into the town. Almost at once, we came across the River Ness, and decided to take a gentle stroll along its banks. It made a pleasant break in our journey, and enabled us to stretch our legs and fill our lungs.

The last stage, from Inverness to Wick, seemed never-ending, as the train slowly twisted its way, first one way, then the other, calling, it seemed, at every village and hamlet north of Inverness. Having left the little port of Helmsdale, we turned inland to make a huge loop.

Our carriage had a heating fault, so it was difficult to keep warm. Even so, fatigue was beginning to tell, and I could not help nodding off to sleep, only to wake up again, due to the lack of heat, or because the train was making one of its many stops. Eventually, we arrived at Wick, about four and a half hours after leaving Inverness!

6. THE WARM-UP.

Though we were to stay with the same lady that I had stayed with on my previous visit to Wick, my recollection of the house and its location had, by now, become somewhat blurred. Fortunately, B.R., no doubt doing its best to make amends for the lack of heating, came to our assistance. Prominently displayed in the station forecourt, was a map, which clearly showed the layout of the streets. I quickly located the road we wanted, and without more ado, we headed for Breadalbane Terrace.

Having arrived at the house, I knocked the door and waited. I rang the bell, just to be sure. There was no answer! I had already informed Mrs. Manson of the time of the train's arrival, so she would normally be expecting us about now. Perhaps she was shopping, and had been delayed?

To kill a little time, we walked a short distance along the road to a point where it overlooked the harbour. Across the water, we could see boats lying alongside the jetty. Beyond, the small town of 8,000 people spread itself out, like the terracing of an amphitheatre. The stage was the harbour, itself, for that was where the action took place.

We wandered back to the house. Still no answer! Then I found that the door was open, so perhaps we were expected to go in, after all?

Venturing into the hallway, I called out the lady's name, to inform her of our arrival. Imagine my astonishment, when a charming young lady came down the stairs and informed me that Mrs. Manson lived a few houses away - and on the other side of the road!

In my confusion, I almost offered her 'my deepest sympathy', before beating a hasty retreat, and seeking refuge in the anonymity of the road outside.

Anonymity?!

The mistake had arisen because the two sides of the road were known by two different names. Therefore, the addresses of the two houses were identical, except for one all-important word - one side of the road was called 'Terrace', while the other was called 'Crescent'.

Having regained a certain amount of composure, we soon crossed over to the correct house, where, this time, Mrs. Manson was waiting to greet us with a warm welcome, as if scarcely a day had passed since I had last knocked at the door.

We soon met David, a lively, well-mannered lad of about seven. The fact that Monique and I were about to attempt the long walk, had created some sort of impression, for, in the morning, he asked if I would please 'write my name' on a piece of paper.

I duly obliged, adding, for good measure, the words:

"Hope we make it!"

It was a nice gesture on the part of young David - someone actually thought we were embarking on a feat worthy of note, and that success was not beyond the realms of possibility! I decided there and then, that if the need arose, we would make that little extra effort, just for him!

On the morning of Wednesday 13th April, the day our mammoth journey was to begin, there was a clear blue sky. The first job was to get some dog-food for Monique. At the supermarket check-out, I was baffled for a moment by what at first sounded like a foreign language. Scots normally pronounce the 'u' rather like the French, or like the German 'ü' with an umlaut. What I heard from the cashier sounded something like:

"Püi tina bag?"

By careful analysis, observing the young lady's hand movements, and putting two and two together, I gathered that she was simply offering to put the tins into a bag!

That accomplished, we were now ready to go to John o'Groats and get to the 'starting-line'. We found that the bus did not leave until about mid-day, so we spent a pleasant hour at the friendly Tourist Information Centre, picking up odd snippets of - information! For example, the name 'Wick' is derived from the old Norse word for a 'bay', or 'creek'. Many of the place-names in Caithness and Sutherland come from the language of the Viking settlers of the eighth and ninth centuries.

The bus eventually arrived, and we climbed aboard. The bus went on its leisurely way to one of the most northerly points of our island, for Dunnet Head is even further north than John o'Groats.

When, at last, we reached John o'Groats, we went towards the shore. I quickly decided not to start actually in the water!

Like countless travellers before, we gazed down at the water, as it crashed menacingly into the rocks, before subsiding into a swirling mass of foam. It seemed that the mighty forces of nature would perform their tasks into eternity, like some giant machine of perpetual motion.

I was beginning to wax philosophical, but there were more immediate matters to attend to. The moment of truth had arrived! Just time for a photo of the Hotel and the Last House, while Monique, off the lead for a few precious moments, investigated what appeared to be a deserted ticket booth, and then we both turned towards the south, and began to walk.

So - this was it! We were away! The challenge had begun! Surely, there could be no turning back this time, could there? I had put in the training, my feet were toughened, I had strong, protective footwear, and I had a well-designed, waterproof coat. In other words, I had rectified all the faults and weaknesses which had brought about my downfall on two previous occasions. What is more, this time, I was joined by a faithful four-footed companion, and who knew what a difference that might make.

There were no great cheering crowds to wave us off - not one single soul! Did it matter? I had set myself a challenge, and that was reason enough to make the effort. As for Monique, she was motivated by a sense of togetherness.

"Where you go, there go I!" was her motto.

The long narrow road climbed gently, away from the coast. John o'Groats was behind us, as we made our way with calm resolve - no hurry, no worry!

Caithness is, by and large, quite a flat area, so we should have time to loosen up our joints, before coming to grips with the hills of Sutherland.

It was very peaceful and quiet, so Monique and I had the A9 to ourselves for long stretches, which enabled us to look around and enjoy the scenery.

"Where you go, there go I!"

For the want of something to occupy my mind, I started to take note of the amount of time which elapsed between the passing of vehicles, not worrying about the direction from which they came. Sometimes, there was an interval as long as eleven minutes!

I then turned to registration numbers, trying to discover the local ones, from the frequency with which certain letters appeared. This sort of pastime helped to maintain concentration and delay the possible onset of boredom. Suddenly, a car came by, the number of which was completely different from all the others. It was a German registration, and we had no doubt seen our first foreign tourists.

Just beyond the half-way point, at the village of Keiss (pronounced Keess), we took a break. One of my plans had been to have a ready stock of chocolate biscuits and cereal crunch bars available for when I needed a boost of energy. I called them our 'emergency rations', and now was a good time to put them to the test. Monique thought that this was one of my better ideas!

The amount of traffic on the road had increased, and when we got to Reiss (which, of course, is pronounced Reess), the volume of traffic was again increased by a steady flow of vehicles to and from Thurso. It was fortunate that, for the last three miles into Wick, we had a footpath to give us some protection from the heavy traffic.

Jokingly, I had referred to the 17 miles from John o'Groats to Wick as the 'warm-up' - or a little gentle exercise to loosen up the muscles, before embarking on an athletic event proper, but a slight stiffening of the thigh muscles, as we tackled the last three miles, told me that they had done just about enough for the first day.

We had done the first stage in 5h. 1m., not that the time mattered. The important thing was that we felt fit enough to set off again, with a fair amount of confidence, the next morning. This would be a real test, a 26-mile stage, for the first time with a full pack!

7. SHOCKS IN STORE!

We had enjoyed a good night's sleep and were preparing to start out on the second stage of our planned adventure. When we were almost ready to leave, Mrs. Manson called out:

"Don't go without your maps!"

I must have beén in a hurry to get on the road, but to leave behind what was perhaps the most important piece of equipment - a transparent plastic folder, containing all my maps and details of the route - well! I wonder how far we should have gone, before they were missed.

Hoping that nothing else had been overlooked, we quickly headed for the A9 and turned towards the south-west. We were in a fairly good mood as we followed closely the eastern coastline of Scotland.

"Just keep the North Sea on your left, and you can't go wrong!"

Those were the instructions I gave myself.

As before, we were met by a cold wind, but the sun was shining. We found these conditions ideal for walking.

We were in a part of Scotland which is only sparsely populated, and there was little to distract us, or slow down our progress, as we passed through tiny communities, such as Thrumster and Lybster. So far, things had gone more or less according to plan, but when we decided to stop for a break, at Latheron, after doing about 17 miles, it was not the sort of break I had intended!

My camera was in a leather case which I carried, hanging by a strap from my neck, so that it was ready for instant use. Unfortunately, when I tried to remove my ruck-sack, the straps became entangled, and the one on the camera case broke. From now on, I should have to carry my camera either in my hand, or in the ruck-sack.

I once suggested to Monique, hopefully, that perhaps she might like to carry the camera, but she would have none of it! Her feelings on the matter seemed to be:

"No, you brought the thing, so you carry it!"

Although this was the first day with a full load, we were not doing too badly. Fatigue was now beginning to tell, however. It was taking a lot more effort to produce the same result. There was a heaviness in my legs, and my stride was becoming shorter. Monique still seemed to be in fine fettle, but we both needed refreshment.

I had planned to obtain light refreshment, especially liquid, every five or six miles, but of course, this was not always possible, if towns and villages were widely scattered.

As well as tiredness, I now became aware of a discomfort at a point between the shoulder and the collar-bone. It was the point which seemed to be carrying most of the weight of the ruck-sack. In order to relieve the pressure, I varied the position of the strap occasionally, sometimes supporting the sack with my left hand behind my back.

We hardly noticed the massive road-works, taking place in Dunbeath, for we were now in urgent need of something to drink. I was informed of a petrol station, a mile or two ahead, where tea was also served.

Having reached the filling station, in Borgue, we found the owner a friendly person, only too willing to serve us tea. When I mentioned the road-works in Dunbeath, he explained that a road bridge was being built, to improve the flow of traffic through Dunbeath. It was something which had been on the cards for years. A photograph in a newspaper showed the bridge in the course of construction.

While enthusing over the marvels of modern engineering and the ever changing face of Britain, neither of us noticed that Monique had quietly slipped into the inner sanctum of the shop - that is, until she suddenly reappeared with a bone, which she promptly chewed to pieces - before our very eyes! How embarrassing!

Apparently, she had struck a deal
with the owner's dog.

Apparently, she had struck a deal with the owner's dog. I was soon to discover that Monique was a born explorer, and an investigator extraordinary! Public or private quarters, they were all the same to her! I sometimes wondered if, before I came to know her, she had worked for the C.I.D.

We arrived at Newport, a small community near Berriedale, where our new hosts, Mr. and Mrs. Steven, were waiting to meet us, at around 6.30. They gave us a warm welcome, but apologised that they would be going out for a while. I promised to keep the fire going, and, in the meantime, I would take a bath. Monique looked at her first coal fire in wonderment, but found it not unpleasant!

I had just finished my bath, when the whole house, without warning, was plunged into darkness! Eventually, I managed to find my way to the lounge, where the fire was still flickering. After placing some coal on the fire, I sat down on a settee, and waited.

The scene was all set for some tense dramatic action to take place. Monique was as mystified as I. At first, I suspected the butler, but it was probably wise not to let my imagination run riot!

After a while, we could hear strange noises coming from outside. I felt more secure, when Monique took up the qui vive position, a daunting sight for any intruders.

Intruders? No - it was simply Mr. and Mrs. Steven, who had arrived back home. They apologised for the failure of the lighting, immediately restored the electricity, and explained that the supply was occasionally cut off by an automatic safety device.

Mrs. Steven had prepared a vegetable quiche for my meal, and it was all the more enjoyable because of the healthy appetite that always comes after a day's walking.

It was the first time we had stayed on a Scottish croft, and it was an experience we both enjoyed. Mr. Steven kept sheep, helped by his two collies, who usually stayed in the byre. For Monique, it was not a case of minding sheep, but rather, minding her p's and q's. Her instinct was to chase almost anything that moved, so every time we had passed a field with sheep (and that was most of them), she had become excited. Unaware of the rules, and unfamiliar with a sheep-farming environment, she would no doubt have created a fair amount of chaos, given half a chance!

The proprietor of one of the hotels at which we called, pointed out that dogs seen in a field with sheep were usually immediately shot - and any questions were asked later! The remark was intended to be friendly, for he was a lover of dogs, and would not like it to happen to Monique.

As we walked, most of the time, within feet of passing cars, it was essential to keep Monique under tight control, and in any case, I should not allow her to be loose when there were sheep about.

8. THREE FINE DAYS.

As we prepared to set off for Brora, a small village 22 miles away, Mrs. Steven, very thoughtfully, packed a lunch.

"There's nothing between here and Helmsdale," she informed me.

This meant we should have to do about ten or eleven miles before we were able to obtain liquid refreshment.

The lunch prepared by Mrs. Steven was very substantial and included a large, juicy pear which, alone, probably weighed a couple of pounds or more! For my part, I was weighing up the pros and cons of increasing my load, which was already heavy enough.

We were about half way to Helmsdale, when the pros came out on top. A grassy bank by the roadside seemed the ideal place to pause and have a picnic. Passing motorists must have been very envious, as Monique and I sat there enjoying our lunch.

Revived in body and soul, we continued our advance into a southerly wind. A blister, which had developed towards the end of the second day, was not causing too much of a problem.

At last, we came to a picturesque little fishing village, with grey stone cottages - we had reached Helmsdale. Now, we had not only the sea on our left, but also the railway line. We had stopped here briefly, on our uncomfortable train journey north, three days earlier. Yes, already three days had passed - three fine days.

A harsh, moorland landscape stretched away to our right, as we left Helmsdale behind. Its aspect would no doubt vary considerably, with the changes in the atmosphere, much to the delight of landscape painters and photographers. Away in the distance, the sharp profile of the hills was softened and confused by the haar - the mist and low cloud blown in from the North Sea.

We had no more villages to go through - just an occasional isolated hamlet. In a letter, Mrs. Ballantyne had explained that Clynelish Farm, where we were to spend the night, was on the north side of Brora. There was a sign-post to direct us from the A9, and we should see a large grey house, on the right.

As we approached the end of the stage, I spotted several large grey houses, and each one made me wonder, but the sign-post was unmistakable. It directed us along a quiet country road, which veered right and passed through some clumps of trees, before eventually leading us to the house, which was, itself, sheltered by tall trees, in a secluded setting.

Mrs. Ballantyne, though claiming not to be an expert, had obviously taken some delight in concocting various vegetarian dishes, and insisted that I should "try something of everything", in order to give a balanced verdict. I was going to be some sort of a pig - well, a guinea-pig, at least! However, the task was not too demanding, since I was now burning up a lot more calories than usual, and there was not a lot wrong with my appetite! I congratulated Mrs. Ballantyne on her ingenuity and recorded a unanimous verdict of "Not guilty!"

By now, Monique had grown accustomed to the new routine of walking, during the day, and spending each night in a different place. As she is a very sociable dog, who loves making friends wherever she goes, she was able to make new friends, every night! Of course, having covered sixty-five miles in three days, she was now beginning to be regarded with some awe, and received that little extra care and attention.

When it became known that, the next day, we were heading for Ardgay (pronounced Ardguy), it was suggested that, just beyond a place known as Mound, we should leave the busy A9 and go by a quiet, inland road, which would take us back to the A9, at Bonar Bridge.

As a matter of fact, I had already considered this minor road, as a possible alternative. Looking at the map again, I could detect no great difference in mileage, whichever way we went, so I decided to follow the advice of my fellow guests, and take the quieter road.

Having finalised our plans, we retired to the realm of Morpheus, to restore our strength for the morrow.

9. THE MONSTER.

The 16th April was a Saturday. Now Saturdays are something special – they are not just ordinary, Monday-to-Friday, working days – Saturdays are days when sport takes centre stage.

Over the years, as a member of Birchfield Harriers, and the Midland Veterans' Athletic Club, many of my Saturdays have been spent practising athletics, mainly distance running. Though, to put it mildly, there was never any danger that I should cause trouble for the compilers of record books, I have always enjoyed taking part.

Sport is for everybody – not just an élite. As the founder of the modern Olympics, Baron Pierre de Coubertin, said, the be-all and end-all of sport is not simply a matter of winning – the most important thing is to take part. Of course, it would also be nice to win, occasionally!

This very day would see football matches taking place, all over the country. This was the day when hearts would beat faster, and legs would ache, a day when every tactic would be tried, when every muscle would be strained and every ounce of wit employed in healthy competition, for the glory of sport.

As I contemplated all the effort that would be spent that afternoon on playing-fields all over Britain, some of the sense of excitement, the spirit of competition and the will to win, rubbed off onto my shoulders. This day, we should not be alone, Monique and I – we should be joined by thousands of others!

There was a difference, of course. Whereas most contestants in the day's events would be competing against each other, whether in teams, or as individuals, Monique and I would be competing against natural forces, the elements and the environment.

Turning to the other member of my team, I suggested how a change in tactics might be to our mutual benefit. In short, it would be better if we both pulled together ... and in the same direction! I realised, of course, that this would be extremely difficult for Monique, with all the distractions to the right and to the left.

It was time to go. Saying good-bye to Mrs. Ballantyne, we made our departure from the cloistered calm of Clynelish, and headed straight for the centre of Brora. From my two previous visits to the small town, one particular feature had remained in my memory. In the middle of the town was a rectangular column, built of rustic stone. Directly facing anyone coming from the north, and mounted about ten feet high, was a clock.

It would be better if we both pulled together ... in the same direction!

On my last visit, I had met two young rogues near the stone column. As I was passing, with the clock immediately above my head, one of them, with a twinkle in his voice, had asked the time. How strange! I assume he had wanted to be sure that the clock on the column was correct.

This time, Brora was almost deserted, so we went quietly on our way via the coast road. About five miles on, we came to Golspie, another of these small but thriving communities.

We were now meeting a fair amount of traffic, as we made our way to Mound, four miles further on, but it was not causing us too many serious problems. The place seemed to be well-named, for, rising high above the road, and overlooking Loch Fleet, was a huge rocky prominence. Here was another section of the A9 undergoing massive reconstruction.

Of course, it is impossible to go many miles in the United Kingdom, before coming across roadworks. Whenever we came to them, we gratefully accepted the opportunity to walk within the coned-off area, enjoying the segregation from the traffic, albeit for a limited distance only.

Just beyond Mound, on our right, was the alternative route which we had decided to use, the night before. It was a narrow track, and hardly suitable for vehicles, so it offered welcome peace and tranquility. The track began to climb, amid lush vegetation, and soon, we found ourselves in a nature reserve.

Young silver birch trees were covered, almost completely, with some pastel green decoration, presumably lichen, so that they looked somewhat like Christmas trees draped in tinsel. The overall effect was that of a fairy-tale forest! A certain amount of mist hung over the hills, adding to the enchantment of the scene.

Meanwhile, not always visible, but always audible, was the rippling and babbling Strath Carnaig, trickling, sometimes cascading its way from Loch Buidhe. Included in the orchestration, were many bird-calls, which I could not recognise. I thought of my ornithological friends, for whom this place would, no doubt, have been paradise!

In the undergrowth, near the water, I occasionally caught a glimpse of mallards, wild mallards in their natural habitat, and unlike the tame ducks we were used to feeding, back at home.

We had gone some miles in these blissful surroundings, when I heard a car approaching from behind. As it passed, it slowed down, and one of its occupants enquired, in a Scottish accent:

"Are we on the right road for Loch Buidhe?"

I assured the gentlemen that they were - and then felt it was a bit of a nerve for a Sassenach to direct a Scotsman to his own Loch!

We continued our gentle climb, and eventually, Loch Buidhe appeared on our right - as did the two Scotsmen who had passed us earlier.

We seemed to have been climbing for a long time, and I wondered how long it would be before we started to go down. About a mile away to our right, was Beinn Donouill, 1144 feet above sea level.

Beyond the Loch, the track bore to the left and, as expected, began to descend towards Bonar Bridge. It was now late afternoon, and all was peaceful and still. Suddenly, a strange animal, dark brown or black, cat-like, yet too large to be a cat, came out of the hedge, on our left, about 80 yards ahead, and loped down the lane for about 30 yards, before disappearing through an open gate on the right. Monique had not noticed anything unusual ahead, having been distracted by something in the hedge at the side of the road.

At last, I suspected that we must be getting close to Bonar Bridge. We had enjoyed our escape into solitude, and our discovery of the beauty and the wonders of nature in the wild, but we were not too sorry when we saw signs of civilisation. Having been a teacher for much of my life, I should not normally have found a road-sign indicating the proximity of a school particularly alluring, but the silhouettes of two children on the sign ahead seemed to say:

"Welcome back to the world of human beings!"

After Bonar Bridge, we had a pleasant stretch of about a mile, with the water of the Dornoch Firth on our left, before reaching Ardgay.

We had completed the day's stage, but we were about four and a half miles from Corvost, where we were to spend the night. I had arranged to telephone Mr. Munro, who would have come to collect us in his car, but I felt we were capable of doing these last few miles, though obviously not bubbling with energy. I enquired the way a couple of times, but I still managed to take a wrong turning.

The farther we went along the beautiful Strath Carron, the narrower and quieter became the road. The last mile was so quiet, I decided that it would be safe to let Monique off the lead. The moment she was loose, she started to chase rabbits, which inhabited the banks and hedgerows at the side of the road.

What amazed me was the fact that she still had this energy left, at the end of a 32-mile walk! To think that I had wondered how her stamina would cope with these long distances! Indeed, it was more a question of whether my own stamina would be equal to the task.

On his croft, besides keeping cattle and sheep, Mr. Munro also grew the vegetables for Mrs. Munro's excellent home cooking.

When I asked Mrs. Munro if she could recommend a simple, vegetarian dish, she suggested 'skirlie', or 'skirlie-in-the-pan'. 'Skirlie' means 'sizzling' - the noise made by frying. The recipe is based on a popular traditional Scottish recipe, intended for a meatless day.

For two people, take: 4 oz. medium oatmeal,
1 or 2 onions,
2 oz. vegetable fat,
and salt, to taste.

Melt the fat and brown the onion slices. Add the oatmeal, stirring continually, on a medium heat, for seven to ten minutes, till thoroughly cooked. It is best served with mashed and buttered potatoes, and mashed swede, buttered and peppered.

During the evening, I mentioned the mysterious creature I had seen, that afternoon. Apparently, there had already been one or two sightings of strange beasts and, in fact, one of them had been caught, and was the subject of a scientific investigation. Such animals would obviously not be very popular with the sheep farmers!

10. MUSIC & MEDITATION.

Our journey from Clynelish to Corvost had been very eventful, so we had no difficulty in getting to sleep. If we had had any problem, there were plenty of sheep in the neighbourhood, just waiting to be counted.

In the morning, Mr. Munro drove us into Ardgay, where we said good-bye. I set my ruck-sack squarely on my back, and we set off at once for Dingwall, 26 miles off.

We stayed on the A9 for nearly four miles, following the coast-line of the Dornoch Firth, as far as Fearn Lodge. At this point, we branched off to the right, taking to the hills, on the A836. The climb was quite sharp for two miles, over Struie Hill, 1218 feet above sea level, at its highest point, though the road rose not much more than 700 feet.

"No problem - we've done it all before," I told myself.

As for Monique, she was still enjoying the great adventure, and the novelty of it all.

It was a pity that she had to be on the lead almost the whole time. Unfortunately, she did not appreciate the danger of traffic - the rules of the road were foreign to her. She placed much more importance on the smells and movements in the vegetation alongside the road. Quite often, without warning, she would pull to the right, having detected a sheep, a rabbit, or some other creature. Distractions of this sort would at once trigger off an instinctive reaction to turn and chase. There was a risk that she might pull to the opposite side of the road, in the face of the oncoming traffic, so, at times, a very short lead was essential.

Generally speaking, drivers, especially the long-distance transport drivers, drove with skill and courtesy, and we were grateful to them for tolerating our presence on the road, when no footpath was available. We apologise sincerely, if there were times when we made matters difficult, or added to problems already existing, due to the nature of the road and the volume of the traffic.

There were a few occasions when a motorist would overtake a vehicle behind us, and in so doing, would cross to our side of the road, missing us by inches! The fact that it happened so rarely, made it all the more dangerous, though it did help to relieve the monotony!

We were now over the crest of the hill. Ahead, lay twelve miles of road across the wild open moor of Easter Ross. The only means of liquid refreshment would be at Aultnamain Inn, after about three miles. When I had last crossed the moor, I had called at the Inn and asked jokingly if I could 'fill up with a pot of tea'. The landlord had not been amused!

This time, he was not even there - the Inn had closed, presumably, due to lack of business. This was naturally a bit of a blow for both of us - or all three of us! Still, there was nothing for it - but to press on, gamely. Fortunately, during the last two days, the weather had been cool and damp. At least, Monique would find refreshment in the pools of water, along the way. My 'emergency rations' of chocolate biscuits, and cereal crunch bars, would also keep us going.

A few miles further on, peat-digging, which I had noticed on my two earlier walks, was still taking place.

Eventually, we came to one or two little villages, before rejoining the A9 on the Cromarty Firth, two miles north-east of Evanton. Arriving in the village, we took a welcome break at the Novar Arms Hotel.

Mrs. Lamont, who was to be our host in Dingwall, had suggested that we took the Old Evanton Road, for the last six miles into the town. The advice was good, for it proved to be a very pleasant route, much quieter than the busy A9. Of course, by now, the old legs were starting to feel the strain, and although Dingwall came into view fairly soon, it took us longer than expected to get there.

The house was easy to find, but on arrival, I was surprised to find a note, inviting us to go in and make ourselves at home. It was Sunday, and Mrs. Lamont, who was a keen church-goer, arrived home shortly after.

While she was preparing my meal, I suddenly heard Mrs. Lamont burst into song. She had a pleasant singing voice and was probably going over one of the hymns she had sung, that evening. The tune was quite a well-known one, so I joined in.

This prompted me to consult my list of 'tunes to walk to' - tunes with a strong marching rhythm, which I had compiled before leaving home, and which, I thought, would give good mileage, bearing in mind the space it took up in my ruck-sack, and its weight. The idea was that, in times of boredom, or weary legs, or both, an appropriate tune, passing through the mind, would help to lift the spirits and keep the pace going.

I had already used the list a few times, mentally going through the tunes while walking in step with the beat.

To avoid the need for constant reference to the list, I made a note of four tunes and went through those. Then I consulted the list for the next group of four, and so on. Of course, if the repertoire is limited, there is bound to be one tune that will go round and round in your head, ad infinitum, and eventually drive you mad! I therefore had a long list - and a fairly mixed bag, at that!

There were songs with a French connection, such as 'Alouette!', and traditional songs, such as 'When Johnny comes marching home', songs from musicals, such as 'We're off to see the Wizard', ('The Wizard of Oz'), a few rousing marches, such as Sousa's 'Liberty Bell', certain hymns, such as 'Hills of the north, rejoice!', arias like 'Say, ye who borrow', from Mozart's 'Marriage of Figaro', 'I've got a luv-er-ly bunch of coconuts', and other well-known classics. Provided there was a strong beat to walk to, any tune was fair game.

... 'a luv-er-ly bunch of coconuts', and other well-known classics ...

I don't know whether Monique had a similar list of marching songs - she certainly didn't appear to be in need of such trivia - but, if so, I have no doubt that, high on the list, would figure: 'Run, rabbit, run!', 'How much is that doggy in the window?', and 'Trees'.

That evening, not only did we sing hymns, we also read a section of the Bible. It was a different sort of evening, but a pleasant one. All things considered, I was happy with the way things had gone, so far. By the following night, we should be almost on the shore of Loch Ness!

11. A SCOTTISH PENNY.

It was another 26-mile marathon to Drumnadrochit, our next stopping point. We began the stage with a pleasant walk right through the centre of Dingwall, the little county town of Ross and Cromarty.

The first ten miles would include the three villages, Conon Bridge, Muir of Ord and Beauly, so I was expecting the early part of our journey to be both interesting and comfortable. So it turned out. For the four miles from Muir of Ord to Beauly, we were able to use a footpath all the way. God bless the makers of footpaths, and all who walk on them!

Two gentlemen, who had been our fellow guests in Wick, at the start of our walk, had told me that they were from Muir of Ord. I had vaguely wondered, at the time, if we should get that far. Well, we knew what it was to feel tired at the end of the day, but here we were at Muir of Ord ... and we were still going on!

A mile beyond Beauly, the A9 turned sharply to the left, on its way to Inverness. We stayed with it for a mile and a half, before branching off to the right and climbing steadily, on the A833. Our first outbreak of rain, in 130 miles of walking, did not dampen our spirits. Brockie's Lodge, in the village of Kiltarlity, was a very welcome sight, nevertheless, and we gladly sought refuge and refreshment.

On a previous visit, I had met some Italian tourists. I had opened with a cheerful "Buon giorno!", which seemed to please them, enormously. Unfortunately, the rest of the conversation had had to be conducted with smiles, but after all, a smile can say quite a lot!

This time, as I removed my ruck-sack, one of the straps broke away, having been weakened in the heavy rain. Fortunately, I was able to do a quick repair, by tying the end of the strap to one of the metal rings.

When we ventured out again, the rain had fortunately ceased. After going about three miles along the road, we came to a steep descent. The road went down into a valley, where it crossed a stream by a small stone bridge, and then rose sharply, to climb the flank of the hill on the far side.

We had just begun our descent, when we were overtaken by a car with warning lights flashing. It was followed by a cyclist, free-wheeling at about 30 to 40 miles an hour, and another car, also flashing its warning lights.

I presumed that they were heading for Land's End and would arrive a little ahead of us, as I restrained Monique from breaking into a gallop, down the hill. Still, I didn't envy them, and I doubt very much whether they envied us.

When we reached the stone bridge, we saw a mobile snack-bar, parked nearby. As there was a bit of a nip in the air, I took advantage of the facility, and regaled myself with a 'hot-dog'. To call a hot sausage in a bread roll a hot-dog was rather insensitive, and Monique did not think it very funny! She did, however, enjoy her share of the commodity.

The climb beyond the bridge went on for about six miles. Then came a two-mile descent, with a gradient of one in seven, before the road met the A831, near Milton.

The last time I had made this descent, I had met a French motorist, whose car was having a bit of a struggle to climb the hill.

"Bonjour, comment ça va?", I said, encouragingly.

"Ca monte raide!", he replied - in other words, it was a very stiff climb! Either that, or he was telling me to mind my own business! Zut, alors!

This time, there was no French tourist. It was raining again, cats and dogs, and Monique was even less amused! The wind, for once, blowing from behind, was sticking my trouser legs to the back of my calves, with chilling effect. It was no time for loitering. Even so, I had to apply the brakes, not only on myself, but also on Monique, who tended to hurry down the hills.

The rain stopped as we neared the bottom of the hill and, as we did the last few miles through Drumnadrochit to Balmacaan, we dried out.

We had a little difficulty in trying to find the house where we had planned to spend the night, and actually passed it once, without knowing it. Mrs. MacDonald was pleased to see us. She had obviously spent some time with the cookery books, and provided us both with a tasty bite.

The day had not been without its minor mishaps. Besides the damage to the ruck-sack, the rain had also caused my maps to become almost like papier-mâché, having penetrated the plastic folder. Fortunately, it was possible to peel the maps appart, one by one, and lay them out to dry.

When I came to look through my ruck-sack, I realised that something was amiss - and even, amissing! It was clear that I had omitted to pack one of my polo-neck sweaters, before leaving Dingwall. Still, it was no great disaster - I could manage without it. My pack had become a little lighter, quite by chance, and it would take more than a missing pullover to stop us now!

It was, nevertheless, like meeting an old friend, when the warm and woolly garment suddenly turned up out of the blue, one day, owing to the thoughtfulness of Mrs. Lamont.

Perhaps the most remarkable thing to happen during an eventful day, was the finding of a Scottish penny! As a strong believer in conserving the countryside, I have, after due consideration, decided not to divulge the exact location of the find. It would be a pity to risk spoiling the beauty of such lovely scenery, by sparking off another 'gold-rush'!

... a bit of a struggle to climb the hill

12. OUR FEATHERED FRIEND.

On Tuesday morning, 19th April, we took our leave of Mrs. MacDonald and walked the one mile back to the A82, the starting point for the next stage of our journey. This was a stretch of about 25 miles, which would take us as far as Invergarry. For most of the route, about 18 miles, we should be walking along the northern bank of Loch Ness, so a stimulating experience was in prospect.

The road bore to the right, and very soon, the spectacular ruins of Urquhart Castle came into view. The 14th century castle was blown up in 1689, after the Jacobite rising, and since then, it has become part of a romantic scene. Set against the waters of the loch, and the bank on the far side, flanked with cotton-wool clouds, it just had to be impressive!

Drumnadrochit has a museum devoted to the Loch Ness Monster. A few times, I turned to look at the vast expanse of water, but decided that I should probably have more luck trying to find a needle in the proverbial haystack! Far better to leave the task to others, properly equipped for the job. In any case, we had already encountered one monster, only days before, and one monster should be enough for anybody!

The weather was warm and sunny, and the road more undulating than I had remembered it. However, the scenery was always inspiring. Every so often, we would pass a waterfall or burn, bubbling and splashing its way down the rocks on our right, to pass beneath the road, and then, on into the Loch.

With all this water about, Monique was in her element. On at least one occasion, she has jumped into a canal! I sometimes suspect that her ancestors were all rovers and sea-dogs! On approaching a pool of water, she likes to run through it, nose down, creating a miniature wave, while scooping up some of the water as she goes - somewhat like one of the old steam trains taking on water, during a journey. I tried to persuade her to be selective and choose only the cleaner pools of water.

When we had gone about 12 miles, we came to Invermoriston, a quaint village, with picturesque stone bridges, spanning the mountain torrents. More than ready for lunch, we called at the Glenmoriston Arms.

We were now faced with a problem, which was to become more irksome, each time it occurred, namely - how was I to look after Monique and take refreshment at the same time, if dogs had to remain out of doors? There had to be a solution to the problem every time it arose.

This time, the bright sunshine, and some attractive white furniture

on the lawn, suggested that eating al fresco would be the answer. As it
turned out, there was an unexpected bonus!

While partaking of cheese sandwiches and salad, we were joined by a
pretty little bird, possibly a blue tit, who gaily dropped in for lunch.
I offered it a dainty morsel, which it accepted gladly, and flew up into
a tree. Then I remembered my camera. What a picture I could take, if I
could tempt the bird to return!

I loaded my camera and held it ready to take a shot. Dainty morsel
number two coming up! Lo and behold, our friend was back again. When I
released the shutter, it made quite a clatter. Naturally, the bird flew
off at once, its little heart no doubt missing a beat!

Of all the photos I took, it was this one I waited for most of all,
to see what had actually developed. When I received the print, it was a
delight to discover our feathered friend 'tucking in' heartily!

Refreshed in mind and body, we went on our way, following the chain
of lochs, which extend from the Moray Firth, in the north-east, to Loch
Linnhe, in the south-west, practically slicing off the northern third of
Scotland from the rest. The lochs have resulted from a geological fault
in the earth's crust, and Loch Ness is by far the longest in the chain.

As we passed through the village of Fort Augustus, six miles beyond
Invermoriston, I suddenly heard a voice cry:

"Golly! You've walked a long way!"

I turned to see a lady in her front garden.

"We saw you near Inverness," she continued, by way of explanation.

"We started from John o'Groats," I replied without stopping, while,
at the same time, suddenly feeling quite important.

"Oh - good luck!", she called, and we were gone.

Fort Augustus owes its name to the fort built there, in 1716, which
itself was named after a Duke of Cumberland, and which has since changed
into a Benedictine Abbey.

We still had seven miles to do, before reaching Invergarry. We had
again decided to spend the night on a sheep farm. Mrs. Wilson had given
clear directions on how to find it.

On arriving at Invergarry, we turned right, along the A87. After a
mile, we turned right again, and soon reached the farm, at Faichem, half
a mile up the road.

Of course, this extra mileage could not be included in our records,
since it did not form part of our planned route.

At the end of every stage, a warm bath, or a shower, gave relief to sore feet and aching limbs. Starting the day with a clean pair of socks was the other part of the formula, which helped to keep the feet in good condition. There was always antiseptic cream and dressing available, if necessary.

So far, Monique had showed no sign of trouble with sore paws, I was pleased to say. I heard that the working collies, who spent the greater part of their time in the fields, would have suffered with bleeding paws before they had gone twenty miles on the road. As a precaution, I urged Monique to walk on the softer ground, at the edge of the road, alongside the grass verge. She generally found the grass border far too rough and uneven to walk on. The road surfaces were usually a delight to walk on, but the borders were often allowed to fall into disrepair, or completely disregarded.

13. SHERLOCK HOLMES AND LUCY.

We had now completed our first week of walking. On a map, the part of our route already covered, now looked quite impressive. 170 miles of our journey were behind us, which meant we were well on target, provided we could keep going. We had sized up the enormity of our task. A quota of 25 miles a day seemed likely to test our stamina, yet would provide a goal well within the realm of possibility.

Thankfully, I had not suffered from stiffness or cramp, but fatigue generally got the better of me, towards the end of the day. Monique, on the other hand, never had any problems of this kind.

When we were within two miles of our destination for the day, I was encouraged to step up the pace a little, in order to reach the finishing point, and so recover, that much sooner - always assuming, of course, we had not already gone too far, and I was 'too far gone!'

I tried to convey to Monique the news that we had almost arrived at the end of our journey, when we had less than a mile to do. As I have a habit of talking to her in French, I would say:

"Bientôt arrivés à la maison!" (Soon be home!)

I think she got the message!

I quite often tell people she is bilingual. Once, when I said this to someone, he replied:

"Why, she's got a bigger I.Q. than I have!"

Why, she's got a bigger I.Q. than I have!

I think he was joking.

A 23-mile walk to Fort William was our schedule at the start of the second week, surely well within our capabilities. I had an extra reason for wanting to do this particular stage. In 1973, I had worn shoes that were too light, and had suffered the consequences. Blisters had finally brought me to a halt, at Spean Bridge.

Now, Spean Bridge was no more than 15 miles away, so it presented a very tempting target to aim at. If we could reach Spean Bridge and then keep going, I should have beaten my previous effort!

On fresh legs, we were soon back on the A82, and heading for Laggan Bridge, a village about four miles along the road. We had scarcely gone far, when we saw our first Highland cattle, with their long, red, shaggy hair, and their long, prominent horns.

We were soon to cross the Caledonian Canal. We had already crossed it twice, between Fort Augustus and Invergarry. Thomas Telford designed the canal between 1803 and 1822. Cuts totalling about 22 miles provided the links between the Moray Firth, Loch Ness, Loch Oich, Loch Lochy, and Loch Linnhe. As a result, ships up to 600 tonnes can avoid a journey of 400 miles round the north of Scotland.

We progressed steadily along the south bank of Loch Lochy until, as we approached Spean Bridge, we could see a range of mountains looming up ahead. At the end of the range, was Ben Nevis, at 4,406 feet above sea-level, the highest peak of the British Isles. Veiled by passing clouds, the snow-covered slopes made a wonderful and unforgettable panorama!

So far, the day had offered us clouds and bright intervals, but, as we covered the eight miles from Spean Bridge to Fort William, the storm-clouds opened, a desperate attempt to stop further progress beyond Spean Bridge, perhaps!

Mrs. Ball had described very clearly how to reach our accommodation for the night, Old Inverlochy Farm. At Lochy Bridge, the turn-off point for the 'road to the Isles', we left the A82, as instructed, and for the last 200 yards, followed the path alongside the river. I let Monique go free for a few delightful moments. We had done it! We had beaten 1973!

That night, we had time to watch television - with Lucy, aged four. She was obviously well-informed about the subtleties of snooker, and she later became engrossed in the adventures of Sherlock Holmes - until Mrs. Ball whisked her away, just in time to miss one of the more bloodthirsty and gory scenes!

As for Monique, the box with the moving pictures was something else to ponder over - an intriguing novelty. The programme which she thought was far better than the rest, was a natural history documentary, showing baboons and chimpanzees in the star rôles!

Meanwhile, the maps were again drying out, ready for the morrow.

14. THREE CHEERS FOR THE BRIDGE-BUILDERS!

Thursday 21st April would be almost like a rest day, for there were only 17 miles to do before our next overnight stop, at Ballachulish. In a confident mood, therefore, I judged that we had plenty of time to take a look at the ruins of old Inverlochy Castle, dating from the thirteenth century. We then set off in earnest towards the centre of Fort William.

Fort William, with a population of 11,000, was the largest built-up area we had gone through, so far. Stretching for about two miles, along the A82, it is a popular tourist resort, and an ideal base for exploring Ben Nevis.

Leaving the town behind, we stayed on the coast road, which follows the shore of Loch Linnhe, on our right. Though the sky was overcast, it was not raining, and we did the nine miles to Onich without any trouble. At this point, the road and the coastline turn sharply, almost due east. I now began to scan the water ahead, with eager anticipation.

Since the last time I had passed this way, in 1969, a certain piece of engineering had been carried out, which would significantly alter our route. A road bridge had been built across the mouth of Loch Leven, the effect of which was to make it unnecessary to walk all the way round the loch, and so shorten our journey by about 12 miles. At last, the bridge came into view, so low, it seemed almost to lie upon the water. We made the short crossing from North Ballachulish with pleasure and admiration, and gave three cheers for the bridge-builders!

When still about two miles from Ballachulish, where we were awaited at the Craigellachie Guest House, by Mr. and Mrs. Corstorphine, I was no doubt ruminating about something or other (You get a considerable amount of time to ruminate, on jaunts like this!), when suddenly, I was aroused from my rêverie by someone calling my name.

At first, I thought the news had finally got around, and we had hit the national headlines. There it was in black and white: MAN AND DOG SPOTTED BY BEN NEVIS! or perhaps, BEN NEVIS SPOTTED BY MAN AND DOG! or even, MAN AND BEN NEVIS BY SPOTTED DOG! STOP PRESS - BILINGUAL HOUND DISCOVERS ANCIENT SCOTTISH PENNY!

Before I had time to read on, I was surprised to learn that the man who had called my name, was Mr. Corstorphine. He had driven out to meet us, with his wife. As they did not expect to be back in time to receive us, they very kindly loaned me a key.

When we reached the village, shortly afterwards, we popped into the tourist information centre, and picked up some interesting details about the next stage of our journey.

The Guest House was situated near the centre of the village, almost directly on our route. Because of the shorter stage, we had reached our destination for the day, earlier than usual, just after four o'clock. I still felt tired, nevertheless, and welcomed the extra time available to recover. Of course, a lot of the fatigue was cumulative. Even early in the day, I was not usually brimming with energy, due to the short period of recovery, between stages. It was something that had to be accepted.

In the evening, as we dined, we looked out onto the village street, watching the 'world go by', before taking our own constitutional, in the park across the way.

It was now a matter of getting into the right frame of mind for the big test, facing us the following day. This would involve a long, steep climb, over the Pass of Glencoe, followed by a daunting march across the wild Rannoch Moor, to Bridge of Orchy, a distance of 25 miles in all.

The immediate task, however, was to sleep and regain as much energy as possible, during the hours of darkness.

15. THE PAUPER AND THE PRINCE.

Though we intended to make an early start, it was 9.40, by the time we left Ballachulish. The weather was cool, and there was a fresh wind. In other words, it was a good day for walking, weatherwise.

After a mile and a half, we came to the village of Glencoe, over to our left, but we chose to stay with the A82, which seemed to be the more direct of the two routes. In fact, there was not much to choose between them, since they merged, about three miles up the glen.

We soon began to climb. I gazed up at the craggy peaks that marked the sky-line, to the left and to the right. There were several reaching well over 3,000 feet. The more sheltered hollows were filled with snow, while some of the crests were veiled in mystery, by low cloud.

I tried to fix in my mind's eye the shape of the various hills, and guess where the road would eventually manage to find a way through. The answer to the question was always in doubt, for, as we progressed, every mountain would take on a different form.

Our viewpoint was, of course, changing all the time. Following the line of the glen, our road was weaving its way round the contours of the hills, yet climbing all the way to the pass.

I found it interesting, as I had done on other occasions, to take a particular note of some of the vehicles which overtook us, and watch the route they took, as they twisted their way up the glen. Sometimes, they remained in view for half a mile or more. By this means, I was mentally prepared for the road ahead, having picked out the immediate objectives.

A fairly strong breeze was blowing down the glen, varying in force, with our changes of direction. The sound of rushing air filled my ears, which meant that I had to be particularly alert to all the traffic which came from behind. Nevertheless, it made for an invigorating experience, and preferable by far, to the hot August weather, which had been my lot, in 1969.

Alarmed at the approach of two strange figures, the sheep, straying on the road ahead, would suddenly scurry along, before seeking refuge in the wilderness, to the left or right. Meanwhile, we pushed on, climbing all the time, and I began to wonder when the road would level off, round the next bend, perhaps? Eventually, we reached the pass, which is about nine miles beyond Glencoe village.

The last time I had made the climb, I had bought a beaker of tea at a mobile canteen. It had immediately become the fatal cauldron in which countless gnats had committed suicide! On this occasion, the gnats were not around - but neither was the tea!

We called upon our 'emergency rations' from time to time, but as we still had about 14 miles to do, before reaching Bridge of Orchy, we were mostly in need of something to drink.

A little further on, we came to the only habitation actually on the A82, throughout the whole stretch of 24 miles between Glencoe and Bridge of Orchy. There was no sign that refreshments were available, but there was no harm in finding out. As it happened, we were able to satisfy our thirst, and so be in a fit state to continue our journey.

Had we not been successful, we should, no doubt, have called at the King's House Hotel, which lies about one mile north of the A82. This is reputed to be the oldest inn in Scotland.

However, we were now fortified - and we needed to be, since we were crossing Rannoch Moor, a desolate waste, where, according to the writer, H. V. Morton, many a brave soul had bitten the dust - or words to that effect!

My mind went back to 1969. That year, I had set myself the task of walking 30 miles from Kinlochleven to Bridge of Orchy, on a hot summer's day. The last few miles had been a severe struggle. In the darkness, I had stumbled along the edge of the road, dazzled by car headlights, as I aimed for the lights of the distant hotel.

Arriving exhausted, dehydrated and dispirited, I had been told that there was 'no room at the inn', and had, without hesitation, accepted an offer of a bed in a neighbouring cottage.

The following morning, I had taken breakfast at the hotel. With my waterproof having burst open at the seams, and my ruck-sack probably the worse for wear, I had felt decidedly like a tramp, sitting at a table on its own, away from the main dining area. One or two curious glances had come my way, but I had pretended not to notice them.

Never mind - this time, we had a hotel room already booked. Things could not go wrong. It was just a matter of getting there.

The A82 wound its way between the lochs on Black Mount, and crossed the Water of Tulla, before veering into a three-mile finishing straight, with Loch Tulla on the right. We reached the hotel at ten past six, not exactly fresh, but in pretty high spirits.

Glencoe is always remembered as the site of the terrifying massacre of the MacDonalds by the Campbells, in 1692. I recalled Bridge of Orchy as the scene of my shameful surrender, in 1969. That morning, I had set off and had gone just about 200 yards, before the onset of rain had been the last straw, convincing me that it would be more advisable to go back to the very convenient railway station, I had just passed.

Here I was again, at Bridge of Orchy, and I was as certain as it is possible to be, that Monique and I would be off on our travels again, in the morning. Perhaps I could avenge my defeat of 1969?

Just a moment, though! In 1969, in reaching Bridge of Orchy, I had covered 247 miles; this year, we had done only 235 miles - the bridge at Ballachulish had removed 12 miles from our route. Strictly speaking, we had to do at least 13 miles the following day, before vengeance could be claimed.

I went down to the dining-room for my evening meal. Where were all the other guests? I had the whole dining-room to myself! I gazed round and tried to picture the scene as it had been, that morning in 1969. It was over there, by the wall, that I must have sat, I said to myself. In fact, I could not help remarking upon it to the waiter, as he went about his duties, giving me his undivided attention.

Had I been a king, I could not have asked for more! As I dined, in solitary splendour, an orchestra played, and sweet sounds filled the air with subtle harmonies. The music, coming from the framework of the room itself, was a soothing and very agreeable selection of pieces by Mozart, Offenbach, and others.

The waiter brought in the 'pièce de résistence', the crowning glory - a slice of strawberry cheesecake, topped with strawberries worthy of a prince. What a difference 19 years can make! 1969 - a pauper; 1988 - a prince!

16. THE BONNIE, BONNIE BANKS.

I telephoned Roy, back at 'base', to report on our progress so far. Roy and Ken were keeping an eye on the way things were developing, so it was nice to pass on the good news, when there was some.

Before leaving for Scotland, I had given Roy a detailed schedule of our planned itinerary. Each night, on a map, Roy would move a pin about half an inch along the line of our route. Then, from 'HQ of operations' he would liaise with Ken, and anyone else who might be interested in our whereabouts. As the pin made its nightly leaps across the map, it was a little as if we. Monique and I, were merely puppets, or robots, and were being activated by remote control.

The weather was ideal as we set off from Bridge of Orchy, Saturday, 23rd April. A short way along the road, more or less where I had turned back on that fateful day in 1969, I turned round again - but, this time, it was only to take a parting shot at the hotel ... with my camera, of course! This time, there would be no turning back!

Now, Monique and I were both breaking new ground - heading into the unknown, as it were, and this added a new dimension to our venture.

The A82 climbed steadily for about four miles, before dropping down to Tyndrum (pronounced Tyne-, like the river, -drum). Over to our left, was the southern end of the Grampians, Beinn Dorain, 3524 feet above sea level being the highest peak. Looping round the flanks of the mountains was the railway, usually no more than half a mile from the road.

Even at that very moment, I could detect a train, looking more like a miniature model, apparently crawling round the sides of the mountains, and staying always at the same height. That was, without any doubt, the train I should have been on, had this been 1969, I thought.

At Tyndrum, we took our first break, before setting off on a second six-mile stint, to Crianlarich. The road and the railway were naturally taking the easy course, which was along the vale of Strath Fillan.

Very occasionally, we caught a glimpse of walkers who were tackling the West Highland Way. They would have been very difficult to miss, due to the garish colours they were wearing! To see other people out there, miles away from civilisation, was quite an event, in itself!

In wearing such outlandish colours, the walkers had not just fallen for the latest fashion in haute couture. There was more method in their madness, for, if one of the walkers should go astray, he or she would be quite easily spotted in the startling outfits they were wearing.

I thought, at the time, how foolish they were to struggle over such difficult terrain, with all its natural obstacles, when there was a good surface to walk on, close by. When they saw us, on the road, they would think we were just as foolish - and probably more so!

Of course, our aims were very different. Whereas they had taken up the challenge of the hilly terrain and rugged tracks, over the hills and far away from motorised vehicles, we were simply taking the shortest and most convenient route from A to B, which offered a good walking surface. Whereas, for them, time was not perhaps the essence, we had to keep up a reasonable speed, in order to reach our prearranged targets on time.

On reaching Crianlarich, we were delighted to see a sign leading us to the British Railways Tea-room, a short distance along the A85. B. R. had conveyed us safely on our long journey north, a few days earlier, so we could now show our appreciation by supporting one of its enterprises, even if it did mean leaving our route.

This time, Monique was not barred from entering, so she gladly took part in the proceedings - and took part of the proceeds!

In rather buoyant mood, we retraced our steps to the road junction, where we had seen the sign. Imagine my chagrin, when, having walked 200 yards along the A82, we came to a second entrance to (and exit from) the café we had just left! Being lured into making a detour when it was not necessary, was quite against my principles, even a detour as little as a quarter of a mile.

When we arrived at the village of Inverarnan, seven miles along the road, we had completed 254 miles, since leaving John o'Groats. It was a significant point in our journey, for I had achieved what, in athletics, is known as a 'p. b.', or 'personal best'. I had now beaten my previous best performance.

The bar of the hostelry, in Inverarnan, was crowded with people who all seemed to be enjoying themselves, in a lively atmosphere. We joined a couple at a table not far from a blazing fire. The laird was sporting a kilt, the first we had seen, incidentally, during our travels.

I ordered our refreshment, and we sat down. The couple had spotted us near Bridge of Orchy, early that day, as it happened, so I started to explain to them what we were aiming to do.

Just then, the waiter, passing behind me, was on his way to a table next to ours, carrying biscuits on a tray. I am not sure exactly how it happened but, apparently, some slight mishap occurred. As a result, two very tasty biscuits went flying towards Monique, who naturally, accepted them without formality and, I am relieved to add, to the great amusement of everyone around.

... apparently, some slight mishap occurred ...

Buoyed up by our progress so far, we nevertheless had to face up to the prospect of walking a further ten miles, before reaching Tarbet. We planned to spend the night in the small village, situated on the western shore of Loch Lomond. Mr. and Mrs. Taylor would soon be expecting us to arrive, no doubt. After two miles, we passed through Ardlui, and caught our first glimpse of the loch, on our left.

We had been eagerly looking forward to the delight of walking along the banks of Loch Lomond, Scotland's largest expanse of water, as one of the more exciting episodes in our expedition. Well, perhaps it was, but not for the reason I had had in mind.

We were unable fully to appreciate the renowned beauty of the loch, for we had to be extremely vigilant. Coming towards us at frequent, but irregular intervals, were streams of holiday traffic, travelling nose to tail on a fairly narrow, twisting road, with no footpath. There was not a lot we could do, except flatten ourselves against the rock face at the side of the road!

This was one of the occasions when Monique had to be kept on a very short lead, indeed. It was a Saturday, and that was probably the reason for the large numbers of tourist vehicles. We kept going - when we were allowed to, and after doing five miles in these conditions, we came to a place called Inveruglas, which has a hydroelectric power station. Three miles ahead was Tarbet, our finishing point for the day.

When at last we arrived, Mr. and Mrs. Taylor were ready with a warm and friendly welcome. We had walked 29 miles during the day, and we had left Argyll, touched Perthshire, and entered Dunbartonshire. The mighty city of Glasgow was beckoning!

17. THE PRIMA DONNA.

The next morning, we braced ourselves for more of the same - about 16 miles, in fact - along the shores of Loch Lomond. However, I was in a state of euphoria, as a result of surpassing my 1969 venture - so much so, that I sent a picture post-card to my doctor, giving the details and adding that I was cockahoop again! I am not cockahoop very often, may I point out.

In cool, hazy weather, we calmly completed the first nine miles and took a welcome break at Luss. The loch begins to widen out here, until, at its widest point, it is five miles across. The many islands are part of its beauty, and add to the delight of boating enthusiasts.

Trying to absorb some of the holiday atmosphere, we returned to the road, where, unfortunately, the traffic was still fairly heavy. We soon came to a lengthy stretch of roadworks, which eased the situation a lot. Six miles beyond Luss, we came to Arden, which is a favourite resort for water-skiers.

At the end of the day. we should have covered 26 miles, and be only a few miles short of Glasgow. It was useful to have a target to aim at, but, in the main, I concentrated on one stage at a time.

During the afternoon, the sun broke through the haze, so it was the hottest part of the day, when we walked on a rough grass verge along the Alexandria By-pass. Because of this, our progress over the six miles to Dunbarton was fairly slow. With hind-sight, I think we might have fared better, had we taken the old road, via Alexandria.

As we approached Dumbarton, the footpaths were greatly appreciated! Dumbarton, with a population of 23,000, was the largest town we had come to, so far. It lies on the banks of the River Clyde, and is part of the great Glasgow conurbation, though the distance from centre to centre, is about 15 miles.

A medieval castle, high on a rock, was evidence of Dumbarton's long history. In the shipyards, in 1869, the famous clipper, the Cutty Sark, first saw the light of day.

It is said that about one third of the whole population of Scotland live within ten miles of Glasgow. Though we were well into the built-up area, the change from country to town had happened so gradually, that we had hardly noticed it.

Our overnight stop was at Old Kilpatrick, which was five miles from Dumbarton. Soon after leaving Dumbarton, we turned off the A82 and took the A814, Dumbarton Road, sticking close to the north bank of the Clyde. One district merged into another, so that it was difficult to be certain where we were. Once, I thought we had arrived, but, in fact, we were in a district called Bowling, and still had a mile and a half to do.

At our second attempt, without a shadow of a doubt, we had arrived. To prove it, there was Mrs. Newton to welcome us. She soon had ready, a well-balanced meal, consisting of corn on the cob, followed by brown nut rissoles in ratatouille. It has to be said - when it came to satisfying the inner man, our landladies always turned up trumps!

The feeding of Monique sometimes proved to be more difficult. When possible, I bought tins of dog food en route, usually towards the end of the day, to avoid carrying the extra load farther than necessary, but it did not always work out.

On the occasions when I was unlucky, the landladies either had dog-food in stock, having dogs of their own, or provided something which was just as suitable, such as cat-food.

During the day, Monique would happily share whatever was going, and several times, she received special tit-bits, for was she not the 'prima donna' of the circus? Yes, Monique was my leading lady - especially if, at the end of the day, I tended to flag a little.

It soon became clear that she could easily devour two whole tins of dog-meat a day, about twice her normal intake, such was the extra energy she was burning up! She was worth every ounce!

18. A CLEAN PAIR OF HEELS.

Monday 25th April was the warmest day we had had, so far. However, the 20 miles right through the centre of Glasgow, to High Blantyre, were sure to be interesting, and would provide flat walking, and footpaths.

As we left Old Kilpatrick, I glanced back at the road bridge, which was carrying a constant stream of fast-moving traffic, at a considerable height. This was the Erskine Bridge, which we had seen sign-posted many times, the previous day, and which had roused my curiosity. It was long and slender, and by spanning the A814 and the River Clyde, it provided a link between the A82 and the M8 motorway, just beyond Erskine.

We were soon passing the Clydebank shipyards, where the great ocean liners were built - the Queen Mary and the Queen Elizabeth. In planning our route, I had relished the chance to go through what was possibly the greatest centre of shipbuilding in the world.

I recalled the years of glamour and glory, when the ocean giants of France and the United Kingdom would vie with each other in the bid to be the fastest to cross the Atlantic, and so hold the Blue Riband. As time went by, things changed, of course. There were years when there were no new ships required, and the yards were plunged into gloom and misery.

Onward we went, drawn to the city centre, as if by a magnet. As we reached Kelvingrove, we passed the Kelvin Hall on our right, and, on our left, one of Scotland's tourist attractions, the Art Gallery and Museum.

We turned into Sauchiehall Street. The name was very familiar, and I was not sure what to expect. For some reason or other, the name had a funny ring to it, and I wanted to smile. It was, I imagined, one of the streets belonging to Sir Harry Lauder, the Scottish comedian who sang 'I belong to Glasgow'. In fact, it turned out to be a long street, so long that its character changed, along its length. It was no great surprise, when we found part of it under repair.

My mind was preoccupied by one thing above all others, at this time - the need to have the heels of my shoes repaired. The outer edges, the parts that made first contact with the ground, were worn right down!

We had gone almost 300 miles - about a third of our total distance. Now, two great cities are so situated that they divide the distance from John o'Groats to Land's End into three almost equal parts. One third of the journey had worn down one pair of heels. I needed a new pair to get us to Birmingham, where I knew I had similar shoes, ready to see us over the last third of our journey. The problem was to find heels that would do the middle third, from Glasgow to Birmingham.

As we approached the main shopping areas, I began to look out for a shoe-shop, where instant repairs could be carried out. This ought to be fairly simple in a city the size of Glasgow, with 762,000 inhabitants.

We tried several shops, as we entered Buchanan Street, a pedestrian precinct, and then into Argyle Street and Trongate. For various reasons to do with the size, or the type, we met with no success. We now forked right, into London Road, and were on our way out of the centre - still without repairs!

I was now getting worried and began to despair, as we left the main shopping centre behind, and approached Bridgeton. Taking the Dalmarnock Road, the A749, we had reached Dalmarnock, two miles out from the centre of the city, when I happened to look across the road. There, on a small shop door, was a notice advertising 'INSTANT HEEL REPAIRS'! Had there been a sudden change of fortune? We crossed over to investigate.

On hearing of my problem, the gentleman behind the counter produced a pair of heels which were not only the right size, but were also almost identical to the ones already on the shoes. In fact, they were the kind used by hill-walkers, according to the craftsman shoe-repairer.

In about half an hour, the new heels had been fitted. Bonding with adhesive and nailing made them doubly secure. In the meantime, the lady of the establishment had provided us with a refreshing drink. They then bade us farewell, and we hit the road to Cambuslang with renewed heels - as well as renewed zeal!

We all need luck, at times, I thought to myself.

Having become so obsessed with the wearing down of my heels, it now occurred to me that I had not thought enough about the wear on Monique's paws. If that amount of synthetic material was being worn off my shoes, how were Monique's paws able to cope? Obviously, any replacement had to be made by natural growth. I tried to find some sort of explanation.

Perhaps her paws moved so quickly and lightly over the ground, that they made only brief contact, with hardly any friction. It is a certain fact that, if and when damage to the skin occurs, nature is always quick to deal with the emergency. Furthermore, when skin is subjected to more than its normal amount of wear, it eventually develops a toughness equal to the demands. Still, Monique's ability to absorb such harsh treatment was remarkable ... by any standards!

At Rutherglen, we crossed the Clyde and headed for Cambuslang. For some reason or other, the way to High Blantyre was not sign-posted, even though it could have been no more than four miles away. According to my maps, it lay in the general direction of Hamilton, and a mile or two off the main road, to the right. Probably, my maps were not detailed enough - perhaps we had somehow strayed off course?

We made a few enquiries, and took to the quiet country roads. This final section of the stage involved a fair amount of climbing. A couple of women athletes, out on a training run, overtook us, at one point.

After more enquiries, and still more climbing, we arrived, finally, at our destination. The 'high', in High Blantyre, had come to have real significance!

The Crossbasket Christian Centre had a character all its own. In a quiet setting, the large white house was situated in attractive gardens, in which it was a delight to stroll. Moreover, the welcome, the comfort and the cooking were second to none!

In the evening, I managed to get a news-flash through to Maisie, at HQ, thanks to our hosts and British Telecom. I reported that we were on schedule and making good progress, though it felt as if we had done more than 20 miles, that day.

It seemed ironic that we had experienced so much trouble in finding High Blantyre, for we were near the birthplace of David Livingstone, the great Scottish explorer, born 1813. The David Livingstone Centre is the place to go, to see his valuable work as a missionary and his remarkable discoveries in Africa illustrated and commemorated.

Here was someone who had discovered the Victoria Falls and searched for the source of the Nile! How dare we make such a fuss about reaching High Blantyre!

Monique and I once tried to find the source of the River Rea, which flows through Birmingham into the River Tame. We were doing quite well, until I suddenly slipped on some wet moss and slid right into the river, on my bottom! I must have looked rather like a newly-built ship sliding gracefully from the stocks. I was well and truly launched - except that I sank, immediately on entry!

Fortunately, the water was only about six inches deep at that time. Monique, who, for some time, had been splashing around in the water with great glee, wondered why I hadn't taken the plunge before - it was a hot day! Personally, I thought it was very undignified to take to the water in such a manner. Besides, it came as quite a shock to the system!

19. A GOOD IMPRESSION.

Rejuvenated by the peaceful ambiance of the Crossbasket Centre, our departure, the following morning, was marked by a certain optimism. The first task was to regain our bearings and return to the main road, a lot easier than finding our accommodation, the previous evening. Soon after joining the A72, we came to Hamilton, a town of about 40,000. Like many other towns, its name had become familiar mainly due to the existence of its football team. My reference is, of course, purely 'academical'!

We were in the Clyde valley, in the county of Lanarkshire. We were finding the A72 a busy road, and were not too keen on the din created by the heavy traffic. Whenever a quieter route presented itself, we had no hesitation in taking it, in preference to the noisy main roads, with the smell of exhaust gases.

Usually, these quiet roads had once been main highways, and had had to cater for traffic of all kinds, having been, perhaps, the only way of getting from one town to the next. Now, they had become outdated, owing to changes in motor vehicles, and the increase in the volume of traffic. They had been superseded and by-passed by more modern and faster routes.

The original main road was now relegated to second class and handed down to the slower moving local traffic, to the more adventurous tourist who has left the beaten track, and to the casual pedestrian, wending his way, perhaps, from John o'Groats to Land's End.

We were happy to leave the A72, therefore, and join the B7078.

The sky was overcast, and a cool breeze fanned our faces, as we did the six miles to Larkhall. As our temperature remained low, our spirits remained high. The mountains were now behind us, and it was possible to see for miles in all directions, across gently undulating terrain. Just over to our left was the M74 motorway, which was to accompany us for the greater part of the day, a fact of which we were constantly reminded, by the perpetual din of its traffic!

Having reached Larkhall, we set about our customary task of seeking liquid refreshment. I made several attempts, at bars and cafés, without success, for Monique was always refused entry. I was not going to leave her tied up, out of sight, for more than a few seconds. so there did not seem to be an answer to the problem.

I began to despair, and we had almost decided to leave for the next town, when a friendly local, on hearing of our plight, came to our help. So impressed was he by what we were attempting to do, that he took us to a nearby pub, called The Machan, where he spoke of us so highly, that we were more or less obliged to receive a very warm welcome. Monique again came in for some special treatment and was given some meaty bones, which she tackled with great relish.

A friendly local, on hearing of our plight, came to our help.

With our tanks filled and our batteries recharged, we felt ready to clock up a few more miles, so off we went again, along the B7078. About five miles on, we passed through two villages in quick succession, first Blackwood, then Kirkmuirhill. It was all very peaceful, and no problems occurred until, after proceeding quietly for another eight miles, by way of Lesmahagow, we reached the village of Uddington. Now, on the A74, we were joined by the full volume of motorway traffic.

This, of course, made life really difficult. There was no footpath - just a 30 inch wide hard shoulder - and it was to remain like this for many miles to come! During the whole of this time, a constant stream of juggernauts and heavy goods vehicles almost swept us off our feet!

After about six miles of these conditions, we should be turning off to the right, along a country road, leading to Crawfordjohn. Mrs. Hodge was expecting us, at Craighead Farm, in the vale of Duneaton Water, near Drake Low. Low, indeed! 1586 feet above sea level, if you don't mind - or even if you do!

Our turning was just to the north of Abington. Now, as it happens, there are two roads leaving the A74, just north of Abington, and both of them lead to Crawfordjohn. Of course, we took the wrong one!

In our haste to get away from the A74 and escape into the peaceful, country roads, we had taken the first of the two turnings. As a result, we now had about three miles of winding lanes, up hill and down dale, to Crawfordjohn and out again, before arriving at Craighead Farm, leg-weary and suffering the effect of the drop in temperature.

Soon after leaving the A74, I had enquired about the whereabouts of Craighead Farm, and a lady had pointed it out across the fields. It had not appeared to be too far away, but that was as the crow flies, and not as the weary traveller trudges up and down tortuous country lanes!

Over the last mile or two, I was moving so slowly that I was hardly creating enough heat to keep warm, for it had become rather chilly since seven o'clock. By the time we reached the farm, it was well after nine, but we had completed 27 miles.

I suspect that a lot of the tiredness resulted from having to break in new heels. The problem was not the extra weight to carry, but rather the effect they had on my walking action.

Because the heels were not yet sufficiently worn down at the edges, the heel and sole were making contact with the ground jerkily, one after the other, instead of rolling from heel to sole, in one smooth movement. I consoled myself with the thought that, as time wore on, my heels would wear down, thus enabling me to revert to a fluent walking action.

During the day, 'feeding stations' had not appeared very often, and at one point, the need to top up our supplies of energy and moisture had become urgent. Fortunately, at that moment, on the distant horizon, the vague shape of a white building had appeared, and had given us hope. We were not disappointed, for it turned out to be the Star Cafe. A helping of ham for Monique, and sausage, egg and chips for me, went down well.

It was in the dusk of evening that we slowly made our way along the lonely farm-track, towards Craighead Farm. Lying right in the middle of the track, some way ahead, I could see what appeared to be a grey-brown, pebble-shaped stone, about the size of a cat, or a rabbit. When we came closer, I had no doubt at all that it was, indeed, a rabbit! Seemingly, on our approach, it had become petrified with fear, and had assumed this streamlined form, motionless, its eyes fixed straight ahead, with glazed expression, instinctively hoping that, by looking like a stone, it would not be noticed by Monique and me, and would, therefore, be left alone to survive.

I moved Monique from my right hand to my left, in order to act as a precautionary barrier between the two animals, as we passed. Only three feet separated them (five, if you include mine).

The rabbit stayed motionless as we went by, with Monique blissfully unaware of its presence. I turned to look back. The rabbit kept up the act, until we were well clear. The mascarade had succeeded!

I vaguely remember hearing about such instinctive behaviour, in the cause of self-preservation, but this was the first time I had seen it in real life.

Monique has a very keen sense of hearing - the slightest sound will attract her attention. Her eyesight is particularly good in the case of detecting movement. There had been neither sound nor movement. Indeed, the rabbit had given a very good impression of a pebble!

20. RED FOR DANGER!

The following morning, as we returned to the A74, this time, by the short route, a flock of rams came scampering across a field on our left, and lined up along the barbed-wire fence to bid us farewell. It was the biggest send-off we had received! There they all were, fallen in on the parade-ground, as Monique and I did a sort of grand march past. It took an awful lot of saluting!

Once we were back on the main road, we immediately regretted it, as we were now committed to mile upon endless mile of the 30 inch wide hard shoulder. The only thing to do was to grit our teeth, grin and bear it, and press on gamely, as the succession of heavy goods vehicles raced by, some of them holding us in suspended animation.

... some of them holding us in suspended animation ...

Such was the force of the air displaced by the giants, that we were sometimes halted in mid-stride for a full second. Had our progress been filmed, it would have appeared as if the film was, occasionally, staying on one frame for a brief moment, before continuing its normal movement.

Because of the density of the traffic, we could not afford to relax for one moment! I stared hard at each vehicle as it came nearer, poised to take evasive action, at the first sign of impending danger. Happily, this never became necessary. Meanwhile, poor Monique had again to be on a very short lead, and strictly under control.

At first, it was difficult to predict which vehicles were likely to throw us off balance. However, after a while, it was possible to say in advance which vehicles would give us most trouble.

Cars, of course, had no noticeable effect - especially as they were usually well clear, in the outermost lane. The very long, bulky lorries were the ones to create the biggest displacement of air, which would hit us with a sudden gale-force blast! Had I not been prepared, there is no doubt that we should have been blown backwards, onto the rough waste, at the side of the hard shoulder.

Because a vehicle was large, it did not necessarily follow that the slipstream would stop us in our tracks. Quite often, the heavy vehicles would be travelling almost nose to tail, and the following lorries would be in the slipstream of the leader. When this happened, the full weight of the blast was gradually absorbed into thin air. Three or more of the giants, following closely one after the other, would create no more than a cool breeze, and have no effect at all on our progress.

I had chosen the A74 because it was the most direct road, and hence the quickest, but not only did it lack a footpath, it also had important psychological disadvantages. Firstly, the scene changed so slowly, that it became monotonous. Secondly, we could see so far ahead, that we were making very little headway, or so it seemed. We needed landmarks to aim for - we needed to feel we were getting somewhere.

Nevertheless, we did get somewhere! The trunk road by-passed three villages - Abington, Crawford and Elvanfoot - and when we reached Nether Howcleugh, on the boundary of Lanarkshire and Dumfries, 13 miles of road had passed beneath our feet.

The landscape was not flat. At Beattock Summit, the road had risen to over 1,000 feet, while the distant Lowther Hills peaked at well above 2,000 feet, away to our right. Two miles to our left, was the source of the River Tweed, which eventually enters the North Sea, at Berwick-upon-Tweed.

Seven miles beyond Nether Howcleugh, at the village of Beattock, we were able to escape the tiresome drone of mechanical monsters. However, it was only a brief respite, for there were still a few miles of the A74 left to do, before we could turn off to the left, and enjoy the peaceful country road from Newton to Johnstonebridge. About one mile further on, we found Dinwoodie Mains Farm, on our left. We had arrived!

It had been a pretty tough stage of 29 miles, but we were soon made to feel at home by our new hosts, Mr. and Mrs. Linwood. Monique was not slow to show her appreciation, and was soon relaxing on the settee. Mr. Linwood invited me to take off my shoes, and sit in front of the fire.

We were just beginning to feel completely at ease, in the very cosy and homely atmosphere when, out of the blue, the vicar arrived, followed by some of the neighbours!

... out of the blue, the vicar arrived ...

I felt that they must have thought us very presumptuous and lacking in manners, but I need not have worried, for the mood was so cordial and informal.

One of the neighbours happened to be an osteopath and, in the midst of some light-hearted conversation, she suddenly made what I thought was a rather ominous remark. She had been making quite a fuss over Monique, which, of course, she fully deserved, but then she pointed out the state of Monique's paws. One of the pads on a hind paw had a trace of redness at the rear edge!

She advised that the paws needed to be watched carefully, for there was a danger that they could become seriously worn. Indeed, there was a possibility that an injured paw would put an end to the whole adventure, frustrating all our efforts and careful planning!

This was a serious matter, calling for urgent attention. I dressed the affected paw, on the left hind leg. The dressing remained in place, somewhat to my surprise, all through the night, and even while we walked at least five miles, the following day.

That evening, at Dinwoodie Mains, I reviewed the situation.

We had done 366 miles in 15 days, but had the many miles of walking along the narrow hard shoulder placed an unfair burden on Monique's paw? Having to stay under tight control, mainly on my right, would, no doubt, cause more pressure on her left hind paw, and so result in more friction with the road surface.

I hoped that Monique's paws would be able to endure the hundreds of miles of walking that lay ahead. It would be a pity to have to call off the attempt, having gone so far. All the same, I was worried. The next five stages were all well over 25 miles, and my own feet were hardly 'in the pink of condition'!

21. A SHARP REMINDER.

As we were about to set off for Metal Bridge, Monique jumped up, in her usual excitement, for each day meant adventures new and fresh fields to conquer. Unfortunately, in her exuberance, she dragged a claw across the heel of my left thumb, so creating a two-inch gash!

Wasn't I in enough trouble, already? Still, we couldn't hang about any longer - it was time to go

When we passed the house of the osteopath, she came out to watch us go by. On hearing about my injured thumb, she at once found a first aid dressing and applied it to my wound. Now, both Monique and I wore first aid dressings, and no doubt looked as if we had been in a battle!

"Do you think you could follow us all the way to Land's End - with your first aid kit?", I joked, as we finally got under way.

I had estimated the journey to Metal Bridge to be 28 miles. When I came to write this book, however, and checked distances, I realised that I had made a mistake. The distance was, more accurately, round about 25 miles. The error had come about, because of the difficulty in finding a room, on or near the A74, and between the Border and Carlisle.

I finally arranged to stay at Metal Bridge House, Blackford.

Now, according to my maps, Blackford was situated four miles to the north of Carlisle, on the A7, while Metal Bridge was not indicated. The maps did show a village on the A74, just north of Carlisle, but this was called Todhills.

Given this information, it seemed inevitable that we should have to leave the A74 somewhere near Todhills, in order to reach Metal Bridge in Blackford, which was on the A7. I therefore wrote to the lady with whom we were to stay, at Metal Bridge House, asking how to get there from the direction of Todhills.

This, no doubt, confused Mrs. Liddle, who wrote back, with detailed information on how to get to Metal Bridge, when arriving from the south, since Metal Bridge is actually about two miles north of Todhills, on the A74, and nowhere near Blackford on the A7!

I am not sure whether Mrs. Liddle's letter would have clarified the situation, or added to the confusion. In fact, it arrived too late, for we had already left for the far north of Scotland. The cause of all the trouble was the rather strange address for Metal Bridge - more sensibly, it should have been Metal Bridge, Todhills, rather than Blackford.

To end this comedy of errors on a more positive note, I fortunately came across a B.P. map, which clearly indicated Metal Bridge at the spot where the A74 crossed the River Esk. The moral of the story is - when the geography is in doubt, consult the best map available.

We had no doubt about the route we had to take, as we did the first mile from Dinwoodie Mains, along a quiet lane. It was a bright morning, and there was the usual cool headwind. We had just got into our stride, when, once more, we emerged onto the noisy A74.

Here we were again on the hard shoulder, buffeted by the slipstream of the heavy goods vehicles. This confrontation with the traffic lasted·for six miles, before we were able to turn off and enjoy the refuge of a small town, population about 4,000. We took the opportunity to have our lunch at the Townhead Hotel. The town was called Lockerbie. Little did we know that, before the year was out, the repose of this same Lockerbie would be so rudely shattered by a blown-up air-liner falling from above, in one of the worst air tragedies in history!

It was back to the A74 again, for another six miles, before another chance to escape briefly the traffic's roar was gratefully accepted. We were not on a sight-seeing tour, of course, but we could hardly pass the

town of Ecclefechan, without pausing before the birthplace of the writer
and historian, Thomas Carlyle, born in 1795.

I tied Monique to the sign-post, which stood in front of the house,
and then withdrew to a position from where I could take Monique, sitting
nonchalantly, as if she were a frequent visitor to the home of the great
man. This would make a striking photo, I thought.

So pleased was I with my handiwork, I forgot to wind on the film -
with disastrous results! Because of the double-exposure, the citadel of
Carlisle was superimposed on the birthplace and - worst of all - Monique
was parked on a double yellow line!

Striking photo, indeed! It's a bit of a sore point, for when I had
released Monique from the post, I stood up and, in so doing, gave myself
a hefty blow on the head from the iron sign, overhead! A gentle massage
of the scalp eased the pain, as I looked round, self-consciously, hoping
that no one had noticed. If my mind had been filled with lofty notions,
this little incident brought me down to earth ... almost literally ...
with a bump!

I had a quick look at the map, and we moved on - before fate struck
again. For the next eight miles, at least, our way was lined with small
villages. One by one, I mentally ticked them off the list, Eaglesfield,
Kirtlebridge, Kirkpatrick-Fleming and, last but not least, Gretna Green!
It all made for an interesting final push for the Border.

Which particular stride crossed the line was not clear. However, I
did see a large sign at the side of the road, indicating that we were on
the point of entering Cumbria. I checked the time, as if this statistic
were of supreme importance. Roy's watch registered 7.58.

I was spurred on by the fact that we had at last reached our native
land. We had just beaten eight o'clock, and we had but a few miles left
to do, before we should reach our destination for the day. There was my
companion, as strong as ever. I wondered how many dogs had walked every
inch of the way across Scotland.

The final two and a half miles were fairly straight and flat, and I
looked ahead for signs of a river, or a bridge. Eventually, I spotted a
large white building in the distance - our target for the night? Both a
river and a bridge appeared, after a while. Monique was still on top of
her form, and we were going at a fairly brisk pace.

As we reached the far end of the bridge, a gentleman was waiting to
meet us. I looked at the time again. It was 8.35. We had managed four
miles an hour, almost exactly, for this last section.

Colin, the man who had greeted us, led us to our accommodation, not the white building, as I had imagined, but the house just beyond. Colin was our fellow guest. He explained how, with the help of binoculars, he had seen the tiny figures of a man and a dog approaching, when still far off, so he had been expecting us.

After dining at Metal Bridge Inn, the large white building, we went back to the house to look at our maps and make plans for the next stage. Colin was able to give some local advice on the first section, as far as Carlisle.

We went to bed in an optimistic frame of mind. Who could have told what disasters lay ahead?

22. DISASTER!

Friday 29th April was a hot day. The sun was already noticeable as we set off, and it was to bear down upon us mercilessly, all through the day. It was the sort of weather people had in mind when they asked:
"Did you have good weather?"

Well - it all depends upon what you mean by 'good' - good for whom? - good for what? Certainly, the sweltering heat of unrelenting sunshine is the last thing a walker needs, when he is all kitted out to deal with wind and rain, and is carrying a full pack on his back!

My feet were inclined to blister, partly a result, no doubt, of the new heels, which had not yet worn down sufficiently to allow comfortable walking, in which the weight on the foot is transferred from heel to toe almost without effort. To relieve the feet of some of the soreness, and give them more protection, I had selected three pairs of socks, and then put them on, one pair on top of another. Two pairs at a time had worked quite well and absorbed a lot of the shock, so why not three?

It was seven miles into Carlisle, via Todhills and Kingstown. When we drew near to the city, I wondered what it would have to offer. Until now, it had meant little more than a name on a railway station platform. Now, we should discover it at first hand, absorb some of its atmosphere, and enjoy its unique character, for no two towns are alike.

We entered the city from the suburb of Stanwix. We had crossed the line of Hadrian's Wall without realising it! How times had changed! In the Roman era, there would have been garrisons manning the bulwark, with legionaries patrolling up and down. We paused to consult a street plan, as we crossed the River Eden, certainly more like paradise than in those days of yore!

The obvious route was straight through the centre, by way of Scotch Street, English Street and Botchergate. As we penetrated the city, home for 75,000, we took grateful refuge in the shadow of its buildings, from the ever increasing power of the sun. We also made sure we had obtained refreshment, before striking out on the A6, towards the Lake District.

Three miles out, we came to a large island, where the A6 and the M6 cross. There was also a minor road, sign-posted Durdar. I had noticed, on my map, a country road which followed a similar line to the motorway, as far as Penrith. This, I decided, would be the best route, since even the A6 was almost the equivalent of a motorway.

Now, this is where things began to go sadly awry!

The problem was how to get to the minor road. Since it lay west of the M6, we decided to take the road sign-posted Durdar, and look out for further information. Soon, we came to a sign which indicated the way to Wreay, one and a half miles, by public footpath. As it was in the right general direction, we set off along the track.

It was not long, however, before we came to what appeared to be the entrance to a park. As there was no information, and there was only one way to go, we went straight ahead, along the drive. After all, a public footpath can take on many guises. The grounds were nicely laid out with lawns and gardens. Suddenly, a large house came into view, behind trees on our right. I began to have my doubts - but we had followed the sign, and had not deviated from our course.

We passed through an opening in a wall, and found ourselves in ... more gardens! Where was the public footpath?

"There must be another sign, soon!" I told myself, "There must be a way out - somewhere!"

We came to a hedge and, beyond it ... nothing but a wilderness of vegetation. It was decision time!

I am always loth to retrace my steps - it is like undoing work that has already been accomplished. However, after searching in vain for the public footpath, or even a way out of the gardens, there seemed to be no alternative.

Monique and I reluctantly went back through the gap in the wall, in front of the large house and the flower beds, and along the drive to the mysterious entrance. In fact, the whole detour was a mystery!

Suddenly, a large house came into view ...

At any moment, I expected to meet some irate person asking:
"Excuse me, but do you realise you are trespassing?" ... or words
to that effect. However, all was peaceful and still, as if the hall was
completely deserted.

You will probably conclude, dear reader, that I had finally yielded
to the heat of the sun, lain down under a hedge, fallen asleep, and that
the whole, strange episode was no more than a dream. I assure you, that
that is not the case!

Somewhat depressed, we arrived at the motorway island again, having
added perhaps two fruitless miles to our journey, and wasted both energy
and time - two very precious commodities. By this time, I was certainly
beginning to wilt. However, we were now back on the A6 - the lesser of
two evils, for it was better to face the traffic than to be lost!

After four miles, we came to Low Hesket, where local residents very
kindly offered us water ... and did we need it! The road was straight
and undulating. Though I did not realise it at the time - nor would I
have appreciated the fact - we were treading in the steps of the Roman
legions, who must have passed this way many times. About four miles on,

having passed through High Hesket, I spotted a large building, which was on the left of the road.

We were desperately in need of liquid refreshment, and I hoped that we should be able to satisfy our needs at the building ahead. I thought of travellers in the desert, who see mirages of oases, and are sadly let down, as they approach. Surely, the building ahead was not one of those cruel visions! I stared hard, trying to discover whether there was some sort of refreshment available, or whether the building provided services for motor vehicles only.

It had the air of a large repair depot for motor transport vehicles which had had the misfortune to break down, but as we came close, I grew more optimistic. We crossed over and went in.

The first room we entered was some sort of ballroom, and naturally, at that time of day, it was deserted. Nevertheless, a ballroom with the silence of a tomb, felt very strange - almost unreal. Had we discovered Geoffrey Toye's 'Haunted Ballroom'?

Passing into the next room, we found ourselves in a restaurant. At last, we could get something to eat and drink! There was the bar, but - no barmaid! There were no customers, either - in fact, there was no one at all!

Now, a deserted country house on a lonely estate is bad enough, but a deserted restaurant on the A6, on a Friday afternoon, was too much! I sat down at one of the tables - no point in standing - and made suitable noises to announce our presence. Still no one! I gazed round the room, almost in disbelief. It was a remarkable set - we were centre stage ... but where were all the other actors? Had there been a landing of aliens from outer space, and had everyone been spirited away in an unidentified flying object?

What were we going to do now, Monique and I? How could we best man and dog the planet?

Just then, there were signs of life coming from the back. Snatches of voices filtered through - children's voices, girls' voices. The next moment, two girls came in from what I presume was the kitchen, followed, almost at once, by a lady. The mystery was soon cleared up. Everybody, it seemed, had taken advantage of the gloriously sunny weather to go out and sun-bathe.

At long last, we were able to satisfy our thirst and hunger. I was also able to telephone Mrs. Noble, who was expecting us that evening, at Hackthorpe.

Hackthorpe lay five miles beyond Penrith. Our present location was Baronwood, about nine miles north of Penrith. The time was already half past five. I did a quick calculation. With a big effort, we could make Hackthorpe by nine o'clock, I thought. Was I being a trifle optimistic?

I explained to Mrs. Noble where we were, and added that it might be late - after nine o'clock, when we arrived, but we should definitely get there.

It was six o'clock when we took to the road again, in time to see a cloud pass mercifully across the sun. So now it was a case of best foot forward! In fact, there was not much to choose between my two - neither of which was in particularly good shape! Still, we had our target.

We reached the village of Plumpton, and then aimed for Penrith. It was almost dark by the time we reached the old market town. Stopping to take a break was out of the question - we were late already.

The last five miles to Hackthorpe seemed to go on for ever, as dark clouds increased the gathering gloom, and our resources dwindled. There are times when five miles are no more than a sprint - on the other hand, there are times when they are more like a marathon. This was one of the latter. I was not even sure we were on the right road, and made several enquiries.

We passed through Eamont Bridge and Clifton, drawing upon our stock of glucose tablets to boost our morale, if not our energy. I peered out into the ever-increasing blackness ahead, staring at anything that might be a sign, and having assured myself that there was a sign, attempted to form the letters into the name: HACKTHORPE.

We came to a large housing development, and I asked one resident if we had reached Hackthorpe.

"Just a mile up the road" was the friendly reply, in what must have been a Cumbrian accent.

The road was now climbing, and twisting left and right. At last, I saw a sign which marked the entry to the village. Now for the house!

Mrs. Noble had informed me that the house was the first on the left - she omitted to say that most of the houses were on the right. We were almost on our way out of the village before we came, at last, to a house on the left. With great relief, we waited at the door.

Then came the shock. In the light from the hall, I was now able to see the time. Was it possible? Ten past eleven! Mrs. Noble was, quite understandably, not exactly over the moon to see us at such a late hour.

I have thought since, that all our landladies deserved an accolade,

for the welcome they gave to a man and his dog, suffering the effects of
a day's walking. We are grateful to everyone of them.

However, from my point of view, the day had been a disaster. There
was no explanation I could think of, at the time, for taking such a long
time to arrive. It still took a deal of explaining, even when I checked
the mileage again, and discovered that this stage was the longest of all
- a full 30 miles, and that did not include the fruitless two-mile tour,
round a deserted country garden!

The heat had obviously played a major part in sapping our strength,
but the most discouraging result of the day's effort, was a very painful
bruised toenail. Wearing three pairs of socks, in the hope of providing
a cushion for the soles of the feet, had been a calamity, nothing less!

I contemplated the big toenail on my right foot, as it changed from
red to blue, and then to black. It would probably be a month, before it
was pushed off by the new nail growing beneath.

It was a very depressing state of affairs, but the best thing to do
at that late hour, was to sleep, get the maximum amount of rest, and see
what the situation was, in the morning.

23. THE END OF THE ROAD?

The following morning, I was still debating whether to set off, for
it was another long stage of 27 miles, to Crooklands.

"I suppose I shouldn't really be walking, today," was the brightest
remark I could think of. Mrs. Noble was non-committal. However, almost
as a matter of routine, and not with a great deal of confidence, we made
our usual morning departure.

I had been thinking about my bruised toe - well, if you don't think
about this sort of thing, it jogs your memory, occasionally! The injury
was obviously a result of wearing three pairs of socks, which had caused
pressure and restricted movement. To relieve the pain, it was essential
to avoid pressure on the toe. The answer, then, was to wear one pair of
socks only. As a matter of fact, a lot of the soreness had already gone
away.

The weather, at least, was encouraging - the sky was cloudy, and we
were again met by a cool breeze, mainly from the south. We were already
on the A6, and heading for our first target, Shap, five miles away.

The road was not particularly busy, so we made quite good progress, my bruised toe giving no trouble. On arriving at Shap, we called at the inn, conveniently situated at the road-side.

We were not a moment too soon, for just after our arrival, a coach-load of trippers suddenly descended on the inn, and provided enough work to keep the management busy for some considerable time. Looking through the window, I was able to keep a watchful eye on Monique, who had had to be tethered to a heavy wooden table, outside.

Soon after leaving the inn, we began a steady climb towards the top of the hill, about two miles further on. I was reminded of the climb to the pass of Glencoe, but this was on a smaller scale. Nevertheless, the clouds were hanging low over the hilltops. Occasionally, my eyes turned towards the west where, in the far distance, some of the higher peaks of the Lake District, many over 2,500 feet, appeared to float, vaguely like ships, on a sea of mist.

Having conquered the summit, we came to a long, winding descent, to Forest Hall, about eight miles distant, and then to Watchgate, two miles beyond that. There was no hope of refreshment, so, once more, we called upon our emergency supplies.

Four miles beyond Watchgate, we reached Kendal, a pretty town, with the placid River Kent winding its way through the green open spaces. We crossed the river twice, before staying on the left bank, along the A65. This was a very pleasant section of our journey, for our route was lined with rows of flowering cherries, all bearing masses of pink blossom.

We suffered a minor mishap, when the stitches of the leather handle on Monique's lead finally gave way, under the strain.

It would have been nice to have tea in Kendal, but we were too late in arriving. At least, without a break, we should now arrive at the end of the stage that much sooner.

We still had about seven miles to do, before reaching our overnight stop, at Milton House Barn, Crooklands. Fatigue was beginning to set in by now, of course. Suddenly, we were approached by a gentleman, who had something to say. It transpired that he was a transport driver, and had spotted us near Carlisle, the day before! One man and a dog, walking on the A6, must be rather conspicuous, it has to be said!

He wanted to know if we should have accepted a lift, had he offered one. Well, we couldn't, could we? I explained that we were walking all the way from John o'Groats to Land's End. He had guessed as much.

A couple of times, I had been asked if I hitched a lift when things got tough. Of course, it was out of the question! How could I claim to have walked from John o'Groats to Land's End, if I had done some part of the route with some sort of mechanical aid? This would have been simply cheating, and above all - cheating myself!

Such a lapse would have tormented me all my life. The whole effort would have been ruined by the fact that the rules had been broken. What satisfaction would there have been in arriving at Land's End, if part of the journey had been accomplished by resorting to some form of transport - rather than on my own two feet. We were not on a hitch-hiking spree - it was something more serious than that.

In short, the challenge we had set ourselves was to **walk** from John o'Groats to Land's End, and we should walk **every inch of the way** ... or fail in the attempt!

Time was again pressing, so we tried to speed up a little, so as to reach our accommodation at a reasonable hour. In fact, we were there at about 8.40 - a pleasant change from the previous day!

Milton House Barn was situated in the hamlet of Milton, half a mile west of Crooklands. It had been a typical Westmorland barn, but was now converted into comfortable bed and breakfast accommodation, though still retaining much of its traditional character.

My bruised toenail had survived the day's walking, and there was no further damage. Relieving the pressure had obviously worked wonders. I could not rejoice, however, for it soon became apparent that my faithful companion was now in some sort of trouble!

Monique's paws were showing signs of tenderness, and causing a fair amount of discomfort. This was not good news, to put it mildly! I had, to some extent, solved my own problem, but now, my team-mate was the one in need of care and attention. Perhaps, after a night's rest, she would have recovered.

Alas, on Sunday morning, 1st May, I awoke to find no improvement in Monique's condition. The seriousness of the injury was all too obvious, for Monique was standing on three legs, with her left front paw high off the ground. I could not see how we were going to carry on!

Our hosts, Mr. and Mrs. Jones, rallied round, and telephoned a vet, in Kendal. Fellow guests, Mr. and Mrs. Runnalls, from Cornwall, offered to drive us to the surgery, where an excellent vet, Mr. Geary, was ready to examine the injured paw.

As we had feared, it was painful, swollen and inflamed. Worse than that, there was a cut between the pads, perhaps caused by broken glass.

Mr. Geary gave two injections, cortisone, and an antibiotic, with a recommendation that the patient have three or four days of complete rest and two or three days of gentle exercise, to return to normal fitness.

So ... ... that was that - the end of the road! The osteopath's warning had proved to be, regrettably, prophetic!

We returned to Milton in very low spirits, sadly accepting defeat.

We had given it a good go, but we just had to be realistic. Only a fool, or a hard-hearted villain, would have expected his noble companion to go a step further in such a condition.

Mr. Jones drove us to the railway station, at Oxenholme, so that we could catch the special bus to Preston, and then the 2.23 train home.

While we waited for the bus to arrive, an American lady, who was on a walking holiday, enthused over the English countryside, but, no doubt, she thought I was a very dull fellow, for I was obviously not exactly in the most cheerful of moods.

The bus was crowded, but we managed to get a seat, on the top deck. After a while, the ticket inspector came up and shuffled his way between the rows of seats. As he went by, Monique suddenly let out a howl.

"That's her injured paw!" I said, loud enough for everyone to hear.

I am not actually sure whether it was, but it made me very angry to think that, after all that Monique had gone through and accomplished, to be trodden on by a clumsy boot was her reward! I remained tense for the rest of the journey and, as the bus approached Preston, we moved towards the door. The sooner we were off the bus, I thought, the better!

Fortunately, the train journey was very restful, and Monique seemed to be in much less discomfort. I had already telephoned Will, informing him of our enforced change of plan, and by the time the train arrived at New Street Station, at 4.45, he was there waiting to meet us.

His car was on the forecourt, and soon, the two wounded, one with a sore paw, and the other with a bruised toe, were transported safely back to base, dispirited, but with the knowledge that, in 'retiring hurt', we had done the only thing possible.

END OF PART ONE.

PART TWO.

24. TAKING STOCK.

Spring had blossomed during the three weeks that we had been on our travels. On the little pool, in Edgbaston, a new generation of mallards had hatched, and were busy exploring their universe. Which one would be the first to circumnavigate their watery world, thus proving that it was entirely surrounded by land? It was a time for quiet reflexion.

We had achieved half of what we had set out to do - why not do the other half at a later date - September, or October perhaps, when the sun would be less fierce? Ken, in fact, had suggested something along these lines.

Incidentally, I now discovered that Ken and Roy had planned to make a secret trip to Wigan, to coincide with the day that Monique and I were scheduled to pass through. Somewhere along the road, they had carefully planned to give us a shock - or moral support, I'm not sure which! But, by throwing in the towel, we had unwittingly foiled this excellent idea.

For two or three days, we did the minimum of walking, following the vet's advice to the letter, and as each day went by, things got steadily better. It seemed that Monique was jumping around in no time! In about four days, the soreness had disappeared from my big toe. Both of us had obviously become reasonably fit, as a result of walking, day after day.

I rapidly reassessed the situation. Why not go back to Crooklands, and continue with the second part of our journey?

It was time for action!

I felt that, in a couple of days, we should be ready to pick up the trail, where we had left off. Naturally, several bookings had had to be postponed, already. For the sake of simplicity, I advanced the dates of the bookings by exactly one week.

Unfortunately, Mr. and Mrs. Jones were unable to take us this time, at Crooklands. However, we were able to turn this to our advantage, for it gave us another option. Instead of spending the night at Crooklands, we could walk on to Burton-in-Kendal, and in so doing, shorten the stage to Garstang from 27 miles to 22.

Half a stone lighter than when we set off from John o'Groats, I now had that much weight less to carry.

As for shoes, those I had planned to use for the final third of the journey seemed to me to be the best choice. The heels were sufficiently worn down on the outer corners, to make fluent walking possible.

For more protection, and to absorb more of the shock, I placed some foam rubber arch supports inside the shoes, using a little glue in order to stop them from slipping.

We were now entering a period of warmer weather, so perhaps I could dispense with polo-neck sweaters. There was another way to economise on time and luggage, a small detail perhaps, but I decided to grow a beard.

As usual, Monique had been taking mental note, and realised that we were soon to be on our way again - dogs are clever at recognising signs! As the time for departure approached, she jumped with excitement and joy - we were off on another great adventure!

On Saturday 7th May, we were heading north again, on the 11.55 a.m. train from New Street to Oxenholme, where we arrived at 2.20 p.m. After our week of enforced rest, our energies were restored, our feet again in working order, and our appetite for action sharpened.

We were soon back on the trail - well, almost - there was first the formality of going over the five miles from Oxenholme to Crooklands, the last five miles we had done, exactly one week before. It was remarkable how many details I had forgotten, but which were instantly recognisable, as we repeated this section of the route.

... some similarity to a board game ...

As we walked, it occurred to me that, as in life itself, we had had our ups and downs, and that such changes of fortune bore some similarity to a board game. You might, for instance, draw a card, or find yourself on a square, with the instructions to "Go back 5 miles!", or even, "Miss 7 turns!", since we were repeating 5 miles, after spending 7 days out of action.

We had reached Crooklands. I glanced towards Milton, on our right, and thought of our misfortune, one week earlier. Now, we could get down to business, and start on the second half of our journey.

Not surprisingly, the five miles to Burton-in-Kendal served only to whet our appetite for the next day's walk. Maintaining a brisk pace, we arrived in the small town at ten past five. We need not have hurried - the King's Arms Hotel did not open until 6 o'clock.

The sky had clouded over, and after our exertions, we began to feel the chill wind. Where could we find some shelter in Burton-in-Kendal at 5.30 on a Saturday afternoon? We wandered a short way along the street, and found a grocery store still open. This was very convenient, because it also stocked some of Monique's favourite dog-food.

The cheerful assistant was intrigued to hear about our travels, and offered Monique some 'doggy treats', as a special reward. She also told me about a local mint confectionary. Called Kendal mint cake, the sweet had been used on some famous expeditions, and was highly recommended for replenishing energy and increasing stamina.

The mint is made in the form of a slab, looking a bit like a bar of chocolate. Among the ingredients are sugar and salt, and it has a taste of peppermint. Salt lost in perspiration is one of the problems usually associated with marathons and other long distance events.

We walked slowly back along the quiet street, and at last, the door of the hotel opened, and we were able to appreciate fully, the warmth of a coal fire.

25. A NODDING ACQUAINTANCE.

Having spent a comfortable night, we went out to take a look at the weather, stretch our legs, and size up the start of our next assignment. The whole village seemed to be built on the A6070, stretching itself out along both sides of our route. The sky was overcast. I felt the air to be slightly humid, but the temperature was about right.

Returning to the hotel for breakfast, we finished our preparations, and then set out on the 22 miles to Garstang. This should not cause too much of a problem - after all, we were hardened travellers.

I turned to take a last look at the village. The hotel, like every other building, was constructed of a cold, grey stone, so that the whole village seemed to have a sense of unity. As we looked, the proprietress of the hotel, accompanied by a very young guest, waved us good-bye.

After two miles, we rejoined the A6, but we were now only two miles from the village of Carnforth. It was somewhere about here that Monique struck up a rather unusual acquaintanceship. Another four-legged animal - a friendly Carnforth pony - came trotting across its field to meet the strangers from afar. Monique exchanged a few remarks with her new-found friend, they both posed for the camera, and then it was time to part.

... they both posed for the camera ...

It was just six miles from Carnforth to Lancaster, and I was rather looking forward to visiting the town for the first time. We now had the advantage of good footpaths, as we went through Bolton-le-Sands, not far from Morecambe Bay. However, we now came to a section of road which was far from pleasant!

A two-mile stretch, between Slyne and Lancaster, had recently had a fresh layer of loose chippings. These, naturally, had been scattered in all directions by passing vehicles, and had come to rest on the footpath at the side of the road. The result of this prodigal attempt to keep up the repair of the road was to turn the footpaths into 'torture tracks' - especially for Monique! We overcame the discomfort, however, and safely made it to Lancaster.

For once, we had no trouble in obtaining refreshment.

The county town of Lancashire has plenty to offer the tourist. The name itself shows that the town was prominent in the Roman era. Some of its buildings, an old town hall, and the castle, occupying the site of a Roman camp, are evidence of its evolution.

I was surprised to learn that the population of Lancaster was about 46,000 - a modest total. Perhaps some of the younger Lancastrians drift towards the large industrial cities, farther south?

We had reached the half-way point on our day's journey, so we still had eleven miles to do. We must have felt very refreshed by our rest in Lancaster, for we seemed to make light work of the next few miles of the stage. Galgate was the one small village on our route, and we were soon able to put it behind us.

The going was good. There were no hills to slow us down. However, perhaps the most important reason for our rapid progress, was because we had recovered our energy during the week of rest. All these factors led to our arrival in Garstang by six o'clock.

As directed by our new hosts, Mr. and Mrs. Heaton, after going into the town centre, we first crossed the River Wyre, then passed the church and the Church Inn, to arrive finally, at Castle View Guest House.

Garstang is only a small town, but the Farmer's Arms offered a very good evening meal.

Things had gone well so far, on the second half of our journey, but of course, we had only just begun. By dividing the 27-mile stage into 5 miles and 22 miles, we had made things a lot easier. We should find the next stage more testing, for we might have to do 29 miles in the day! I was, nevertheless, cautiously optimistic.

26. A MUSICAL EVENING.

We still had nowhere to stay, at the end of our next stage, but, in a town the size of Wigan, with a population of about 90,000, finding bed and breakfast accommodation should not present a problem. First of all, we had to get there, of course! As the distance was 29 miles, I decided before setting off, to start looking for somewhere to stay, after we had reached Standish, which was three miles short of Wigan.

The first two miles of our day's quota passed pleasantly, along the quiet B6430, which took us through Catterall, before joining forces with the A6. The weather was similar to that of the previous day, so we were looking forward to some good walking. We were helped in this respect by the flatness of the landscape, and there was also the opportunity to use footpaths, all the way!

Ahead, lay the large industrial town of Preston, where the inventor of the spinning frame, Sir Richard Arkwright, was born, in 1732. We had entered a region which owes its prosperity to the changes in the textile industries, in the eighteenth century. Preston, which has about 170,000 inhabitants, is just one of a cluster of towns which owe a lot to cotton manufacture.

Nicely punctuating our nine-mile advance on Preston, were the three villages of Bilsborrow, Barton and Broughton. Then came Fulwood, now in the urban spread of Preston. Everything went according to plan. Coming to the town centre, we by-passed most of it, on our right. We found the simplest and most direct route was to take North Road, then the Ringway, and finally London Road.

On our way, we happened to pass the local radio station, which was, appropriately enough, called Red Rose Radio. There seemed to be no harm in calling in and leaving a few brief details about our campaign so far, and our plans for the days ahead. I must have been in a confident frame of mind. By now, it was beginning to look as though we might even reach Land's End!

It was hard to imagine that, only ten days before, our physical and spiritual condition had been such that we had been almost ready to write the whole thing off! Was it possible that a change of footwear could be so important? For Monique, had the 30 inch hard shoulder been the major villain?

Not quite cockahoop, but in a fairly buoyant mood, we continued our way through Preston, crossing the River Ribble at Walton Bridge, and set forth into the heart of industrial Lancashire.

The region was in sharp contrast to some of the more desolate areas of Scotland. Almost as soon as we left one community, we arrived on the threshold of another, so tightly packed were the small Lancashire towns! Now, it was almost impossible to escape humanity - not that we were in a hurry to do so.

The place-names trip off the tongue. First came Walton-le-Dale and Bamber Bridge, where we decided to leave the A6 and take the A49. There then followed Clayton-le-Woods and Euxton, at which point, we were about seven miles south of Preston.

At about 3.30, the sun broke through the clouds, and throughout the next hour and a half, we were left in no doubt about its heat. However, we had made a point of topping up our reserves of fuel and water, during our visit to Preston, so we were in no grave danger of running low. The Motel at Charnock Richard was conveniently placed, about two miles south of Euxton, and we took this further opportunity to top up. As usual, it was Monique who got the V.I.P. treatment! This time, her special reward consisted of roasted peanuts.

A glance at the map revealed that we were now only about four miles from Standish, where we might decide to call a halt for the day. Having reached Standish, however, I could not detect any signs of accommodation available. We found ourselves leaving Standish and on the way to Wigan, still without a bed for the night. Well, what difference would it make, if we did three more miles?

We arrived in Wigan at ten past seven - quite early, considering we had done 29 miles - and immediately set about finding accommodation. We were directed to an area where there were several addresses offering bed and breakfast, but, after calling at about half a dozen of them, without success, I began to get disheartened. I was even on the point of giving up and, tired though we were, I seriously contemplated proceeding on our way south. There was still a hotel which we had not tried. This was to be our last attempt!

It was just as well we made it, for we were given great hospitality at the Charles Dickens Hotel, much to my relief! I did not realise just at that moment, what an entertaining evening it would turn out to be!

I was just finishing my evening meal, when a lady sat down in front of the grand piano, which was on a small platform, just across the room. She casually began to reel off several well-known 'oldies' - even I knew 'Edelweiss' and 'Amapola' ('my pretty little poppy'). For one moment, I thought we were going to have a whole bunch of flowers.

"Must gather round, later," I thought, "I could give the old larynx an airing with some of those!"

Plucking up courage, I slowly climbed the two steps onto the little platform and sat down by the side of the piano. I had assumed, that the gentleman sitting by the keyboard had been turning over the music. What music? To my surprise, there was no music to be seen! The only book on the music stand was a book of lyrics ... and that was closed! All the notes were, amazingly, being played from memory!

I borrowed the book of words, hoping to drop upon the words of some of the songs she was playing, and so be able to sing along. I was never able to manage it - she must have had a repertoire of hundreds of songs!

During one of the pauses, I mentioned that my society, that is, the New Arcadian Operatic Society, was rehearsing for a production of 'White Horse Inn', whereupon, the pianist immediately played the title-song and the well-known 'Good-bye!' number! I joined in with some of the vocals, though not necessarily in the right order!

The gentleman at the keyboard then informed me that the pianist was none other than Cynthia Astley, mother of Rick, who had recently shot to fame, with several hits in the world of 'pop' music.

The ivories and the ebonies continued their merry dance all through the evening, as one familiar tune followed another, and more people came to join in the entertainment. We even had a pot-pourri of French songs, including the ever popular classic of Charles Trenet, 'La Mer'.

All too quickly, the time rolled round to eleven o'clock. I had to think of the programme for the next day. We, Monique and I, had just 24 miles to do, and then we should be in Northwich.

Monique, by the way, had been passing the evening quietly, alone in the comfort of her room. Sensible dog!

... The ivories and the ebonies continued their merry dance ...

27. WORTH OUR SALT.

As we left Wigan, at about 9.15, the sun was already powerful, in a clear blue sky. I wondered what effect my late night revelry would have on our progress, during the day. Would I regret having entered into the spirit of the evening with such gay abandon? At least, the lively feast of music would provide sustenance for the soul, and some happy souvenirs for the quieter moments of the day.

Though not quite tripping the light fantastic, we nevertheless made light work of the first five miles, via Ince and Abram, to Golborne, our first pit-stop. Because of the proximity of the towns in Lancashire and Cheshire, there was no chance of becoming lonely or bored. Moreover, we could stop more often for liquid intake. As the sun became fiercer, the intake of fluids became more important. Because of this, we were making somewhat slower progress than on the previous day.

The large Cheshire town of Warrington, population 130,000, was only six miles distant. Having crossed over the M6 and passed under the M62, we entered the town by the suburb of Orford. Going through the town, we gratefully made maximum use of the shadows of the tall buildings, and so gained some relief from the blazing sun. Very soon, we crossed over the River Mersey, and a little further on, stopped to look at the Manchester Ship Canal, opened in 1894.

In my boyhood, I had collected pictures to stick in an album. Some of the pictures formed a series featuring 'marvels of engineering'. The Manchester Ship Canal was one of the 'marvels' illustrated. It had thus created a big impression on a young mind. Now, here it was in real life – and still a triumph of engineering, at which to marvel. With a length of 35 miles, it joins Manchester with the estuary of the Mersey, and can take ships up to 12,000 tonnes.

Very soon after crossing the Manchester Ship Canal, our road led us across quite a different canal. This was the Bridgewater Canal, work of the pioneer of canal builders, James Brindley, and the first canal to be opened in Britain, in 1761.

We stayed on the A49 for about four miles, following the line of an old Roman road, as far as Stretton. We now passed under the M56, before taking the left fork, along the A559. Four miles further on, we reached the village of Great Budworth, at which point, we were not much over two miles from our destination for the day.

Just beyond the village, the road made a detour to the left, but we kept straight ahead, using a public footpath.

"Ah, here comes trouble!", did I hear you say?

Not a bit of it! We had learnt our lesson! This time, our map was equal to the task. It was on a larger scale and had more detail. There were to be no more wild goose chases round mysterious country estates!

Not putting a foot wrong - well, hardly - we headed towards a minor road, the B5075, where we turned right. As expected, we soon passed the Lion Salt Works and Museum, on our left. We had arrived in Northwich.

For centuries, the chief industry of the area had been salt mining. According to the local guidebook, the extraction of salt resulted in the land subsiding, so, in order to counteract the effect of this, the half-timbered type of construction was used for most of the houses. The salt water springs, around Northwich, would make it a popular halt for Romans on the march, for as everyone knows, the Romans were keen on bathing, at the end of a long march. I could fully sympathise with this idea.

With the help of Mrs. Cryer's very clear instructions, there was no trouble in finding our accommodation, and we arrived at around half past seven. A good evening meal included melon for starters. After a day on the march, under a burning sun, what a splendid idea!

What say you, Romans?

28. IN THE STEPS OF THE ROMANS.

Towns are wonderful places to discover and explore, each one with a character of its own, and each one with a tale to tell. They added much to the liveliness of our journey, and compensated for some of the duller stretches of road, which of course are unavoidable, if you are intent on going from A to B by the most direct route.

At the end of the day, we should be in Newcastle-under-Lyme, in the Potteries. We were in our native Midlands, at last! The sense of being on home ground gave a boost to morale. Moreover, having a more intimate geographical knowledge of the region could be of practical advantage.

As for Monique, she was as eager as ever to set out on yet one more exciting episode in our journey of discovery. So, in spite of the heat, we were in good spirits, as we left Northwich, along Middlewich Road.

After about a mile, we came to Broken Cross, a name which no doubt, hides a story. Now, for four and a half miles, along the A530, which is also known as King Street, we followed the same line that had been taken by the Roman legions, about 2,000 years before. A good way to recognise a former Roman road is to look at it on a map - the straighter it looks, the more likely it is to have been a Roman road.

They knew a thing or two, those Romans, one being that the shortest distance between two points is a straight line.

I tried to instil this important fact into Monique, but she made an amendment. Having carefully considered all the evidence, she was of the opinion that the shortest distance between two points is a straight line - until you are distracted by some interesting smell, sound or movement, to left or right. Unfortunately, this happened quite often.

A trace of her route, therefore, would show a fairly straight line, but with random diversions to either side. Of course, the length of the detours would depend on the length of the lead, which again would depend on traffic conditions at a given time.

However much Monique agreed with the Romans in principle, she still believed the extra mileage to be well worth the effort. I have a strong suspicion, however, that this constant tugging is the reason why my arms have grown an inch or two longer!

Because there were no bends in the road, and no undulations either, we could see far into the distance, and so were robbed of those elements of mystery and surprise, which add spice to a journey. Despite this, we knew we had taken the right route, for every step we took was leading us towards our destination, which we should therefore reach in the shortest possible time.

We deliberately took our time along King Street, conserving energy, because of the heat. On arriving at Middlewich, another town associated with salt-mining, we promptly called in at the Cheshire Cheese. Monique was again the star attraction, and was presented with a table-napkin, as a souvenir!

The cheerful landlord was much impressed by our exploits. We had a choice of routes to Sandbach, he said. We could, of course, go by road, but there was also the canal tow-path. In Sandbach, we should also have the opportunity to see two remarkable Saxon crosses.

We walked the five miles to Sandbach partly on the A533, and partly along the canal, since they follow roughly the same route. The presence of canals reminded us, and underlined the fact, that we were now in flat country. In fact, we had been following a flat, low-lying corridor, for most of the way from Burton-in-Kendal!

Sandbach is a small town, with several black and white buildings of timber-framed construction. One such was Ye Olde Black Beare, which had been built in the seventeenth century. A cherry pie, product of our own era, proved to be very tasty, indeed!

We left Sandbach and headed for Rode Heath, four miles away, on the A533. As we crossed over the M6, we paused to see streams of traffic on the road below. It made us appreciate the pleasant quietness of our own road, which converged with the A50 for the three miles into Talke.

Once more, after miles and miles of flat terrain, we were back into the hills - the hilly, built-up area of the Potteries. Newcastle-under-Lyme and Stoke-on-Trent together form a conurbation where around 350,000 people live.

The most famous of the craftsmen associated with the Potteries, was Josiah Wedgwood, born in 1730, in Burslem, one of Arnold Bennett's 'five towns'. He set up a factory at nearby Etruria, named after the district in Italy, for it was from the ancient Etruscan art that Wedgwood derived much of his inspiration, when designing his pottery.

We chose to use a minor road for about three miles, passing through Red Street and Chesterton, before coming across major road-works. There was no great problem, for we now joined the busy A34, with only the last mile and a half to do.

Mr. Stott gave us a nice welcome when we finished our day's journey at Durlston Guest House, as planned. As usual, a special fuss was saved for Monique.

29. FAMILIAR GROUND.

Low cloud and occasional drizzle greeted us, as we ventured out for the start of the 22-mile stage from Newcastle to Penkridge. We had only gone a few hundred yards before we were on familiar territory - indeed, we had actually surveyed part of the stage, when we were building up our fitness earlier in the year. Consequently, I was able to recall certain features on the route, as well as incidents that had happened.

We were soon passing through the pedestrianised town centre, where, on two or three days a week, an open-air market was held. We negotiated the pedestrian subway successfully, where, on the previous occasion, our return to ground level had found us still on the same side of the road!

The A34 has footpaths all the way, so we were able to stay relaxed, and enjoy our walking, without having to worry too much about the events on the highway. With little more than three miles done, we were passing the beautiful Trentham Park, on our right.

The parkland had often been used for league races in the Birmingham and District Cross-country League. Its landscape was as hilly as ever - recalling many a titanic struggle!

A further reminder that we were in the Potteries was the sign-post, in Tittensor, pointing to the Wedgwood Museum, at Barlaston, a mile away on our left. We were in gently undulating country, and the cool weather allowed us to make good progress. About four miles beyond Tittensor, we took our first break, in the small town of Stone.

So far, we had closely followed the course of the River Trent, but, two miles beyond Stone, we parted company. We now began a gentle climb, before dropping down again into Stafford. We felt it was a good time to take further refreshment.

Stafford town centre had become more or less a haven for the pedestrian, rather than the principal route for motor vehicles. We were therefore able to pass straight through the town centre, via Foregate Street and then Greengate Street, where we happened to pass a very impressive building, now used by the Tourist Information Ctre.

Inside, among masses of local information, the leaflets which dealt with rambling in Staffordshire drew my attention.

"They could be quite useful," I thought, "when we've finished this one!" Hey ho!

Stafford, though not over-endowed with gems of architecture, can be very proud of the Ancient High House, the building which we had just entered. The house, built in 1595, was

... recalling many a titanic struggle ...

one of the largest remaining, which used timber-framing for their method of construction.

We continued our way along Bridge Street, and came out of the town, crossing the River Sow, and forking right, along the A449, Wolverhampton Road. Having gone three miles, we passed under the M6, near the village of Dunstan. All that remained, now, was a very pleasant two-mile stroll into Penkridge, our overnight stopping-point.

We reached Bridge House, delightfully situated near the River Penk, at exactly six o'clock, and met our new hosts, Mr. and Mrs. Hamblin.

When I had previously spoken to Mr. Hamblin, shortly before leaving for John o'Groats, I had been very sceptical about whether we should get as far as Penkridge. Now, we were actually here, and looking forward to the next stage, at the end of which, we should be home again, though for one night only!

30. NOT AS BLACK AS ALL THAT!

When we set out on the 24-mile stage taking us back to base, it was Friday 13th May, but who cared? In footballing jargon, we were 'playing at home', and this was sure to give a boost to our performance.

Striding out, we soon reached Gailey, where we crossed an old Roman road, known as Watling Street. Four miles further on, we went under its modern counterpart, the M54, which had only recently been built.

We were now entering the West Midland conurbation of Birmingham and the Black Country, home for around three million people. The name given to the area paints a gloomy picture, for it refers to the smoke and smut of the blast furnaces, the foundries, the rolling-mills, the coal mines and the quarries, which created the wealth of the region, at the time of the Industrial Revolution and later.

Its success depended not only on the natural resources - coal, iron ore and limestone, but also on the grit and determination of its people. In its heyday, and even in my younger days, the night sky would light up with a ruddy glow from the iron and steel works, as giant chimney stacks belched forth flames and smoke into the inky blackness, like clusters of little volcanoes.

All that, of course, is history. Robbed of their riches, the mines and quarries are no longer needed, and nature, with her lush vegetation, and mankind, with his ingenious landscaping and rebuilding, have finally healed the wounds and removed the scars.

The farther we went, the more familiar became the scene.

We made our way along Stafford Street into Wolverhampton and, as we crossed Lichfield Street, I turned to see a banner announcing that, in a few days' time, the Wolverhampton Marathon would be taking place. I was immediately overcome with a sense of fatigue, and decided that now was a good time to take a break, especially as the sun had dispersed the early mists, and the temperature had risen to 21 degrees Celsius!

As we lunched, I remembered the time when, as an art student, I had come to know Wolverhampton well. What had become of all the hopeful and talented young artists of those days? One of them, who was also keen on athletics, and a member of the famous Birchfield Harriers, had persuaded me to join the club, in 1946.

Many milestones had come and gone since then - and there were still many more to come! Perhaps it is better to face the present and look to the future. To reach Land's End, we had to pass about 290 milestones!

We continued our way along Market Street and Snow Hill, heading for Dudley. I had taken the A4123 hundreds of times before, but hardly ever on foot. I wondered how soon it would be before Monique would know that we were nearing our home territory. She kept the secret to herself.

We were approaching Swan Village, and I thought of the little pool, shaded by a clump of trees - the one where Monique had fully appreciated a refreshing dip in the cool, clear water. Here it was again, where the green fields make a welcome change from the rows and rows of houses.

Monique needed no encouragement. She immediately seized the chance to jump in, and splashed around with gusto, in the cooling water. There was a spring in her step, when we once more went on our way!

Our road by-passed the centre of Dudley, nearly a mile away, on our right. As we crossed a canal bridge, we caught a glimpse of an open-air museum, where a typical Black Country village of about the year 1900 has been created. Real buildings from the surrounding area had been brought to the site, piece by piece, and then reassembled to form the 'village'. In addition, there were demonstrations of Black Country industries, such as nail-making, chain-making and glass-blowing, which gave the village a real life atmosphere.

As I gazed at the hill beyond the museum, among the trees, could be seen the ruins of Dudley castle, parts of which are of Norman origin. A zoo has been created in the castle grounds, as an added attraction.

The Black Country is renowned for its dialects and its humour - at least, in the Black Country! To explain the dialects would take several books, but here is just a snippet of the humour.

A small man found himself at the back of the crowd of spectators on the terracing, watching a football match. He made several vain attempts to see the game. After standing on tiptoe and jumping up and down above the shoulders of the tall men in front of him, he eventually became very frustrated. In a disgruntled tone, he exploded with the immortal words:

"Arken say ar cor say, arken say!"

I have used phonetics to record as accurately as possible the Black Country accent. For the benefit of those who may have some problem with the language, freely translated, it means:

"I have reached the opinion that I am not conveniently placed to be able to observe what is going on - to me, that is quite obvious!"

It just goes to show how succinct the Black Country dialect is!

There were now only eight miles of the day's quota left to do. One by one, I ticked them off mentally, as we went along.

About four miles from home, we found ourselves going along at about the same speed as a gentleman, who just happened to be going our way. I no longer had to concentrate on the route, traffic conditions, halts for refreshment, and such matters, as we were so close to home. In fact, so much was I in control of the situation, that it was no trouble to strike up a friendly conversation with the stranger. Quite remarkably, for the very first time since leaving John o'Groats, we had found someone to tag along with! It could not last, of course, and, after about a quarter of a mile, we went our separate ways.

With only two miles left, we called at a petrol station. I had not suddenly been converted to running on petrol - it was just that, because of the heat, I felt that Monique would probably be in need of a drink of water. The people at the shop on the forecourt were so impressed by our achievement that, not only was Monique given water, but I too received a reward - a refreshing bottle of Lucozade. We had met a lot of kind folk on our travels. Of course, on this particular occasion, it was possible that I seemed to be in desperate need of a pick-me-up!

We were almost home, and on the trail of our regular afternoon dog-walk, when we met a lady whom we saw quite often. It would seem strange to see me in a waterproof on such a hot day, with a rucksack on my back, and probably looking a bit weather-beaten, while simply walking the dog, so I thought it advisable to let her know that we were walking from John o'Groats to Land's End, and not just doing our usual daily stroll around the playing-fields!

We were home at 5.20, in very high spirits, of course, and received a warm welcome from Will and Doris. I immediately made a telephone call to the Birmingham Post and Mail, with the news of our progress so far.

During the evening, Roy invited me over, and I gave vent to stories of some of our more remarkable experiences on the walk. He had prepared an excellent vegetarian meal. I remarked that, if ever he was in search of a new vocation, the culinary art could well be his line!

We could not dwell too long on what had happened so far - there was still much to be done. Monique and I had to be awake and on our journey again, the following morning, and I needed to make some arrangements for the final third.

31. A HAPPY ENCOUNTER.

On Saturday morning, a phone call from the Birmingham Post and Mail informed me that a photographer was on his way, and would take pictures, before we set out for Worcester. At about 9.30, the gentleman arrived.

As he prepared to take the first pictures, in the shade of the tall trees, he informed me that he had been a pupil at the school where I had last taught. Well, it's a small world! I expect that most teachers, in the later years of their career, or after they retire, bump into some of their former pupils from the dim and distant past. While admitting that young people change a lot, as they grow older, teachers still feel a bit ashamed for not having recognised them immediately.

Tim, the photographer, went quietly about his work, taking a number of shots of Monique and me, in a variety of settings and poses, and then wished us well, on the remaining third of our journey.

After the lesson in photography, I quickly gathered together all of our equipment and, at ten o'clock, Monique and I were off on our travels again. I had carefully planned all the clothes that would be needed for the last eleven stages and, though the waterproof would be a nuisance in the current heatwave, it would probably be essential at some later stage in the journey.

From the very start, it was a warm and sunny day, so the protection of the trees in the leafy suburbs of Birmingham was greatly appreciated. From Edgbaston to Rednal, we took full advantage of the shadows from the tall trees lining the roads, to escape the burning rays of the sun.

After Selly Oak came Bournville, a name immediately associated with chocolate.

The chocolate is produced in a 'factory in a garden', opened by the Quaker brothers, Richard and George Cadbury, in 1879. So successful was their product, that they had had to move from their original factory, in the city centre, to a larger site, which was then in open country. With the welfare of employees and other local residents in mind, they created a village with lots of space, consisting of a village green, gardens and parks, so that everyone could live in a pleasant environment. In naming the village, they chose the name of the local Bourn brook, to which they added the word 'ville', because the quality of French chocolate had such a high reputation.

As a young boy, besides enjoying the penny bars of chocolate, I had been fascinated by the little pictures enclosed within the wrapper. The pictures had made a great impact on my impressionable mind, feeding into it the wonders of nature and the achievements of mankind - anything from a giant brontosaurus to that great locomotive, the Flying Scotsman.

We had progressed along Bristol Road, the A38, by way of Northfield and Longbridge, and were now passing the famous Austin works, founded by Sir Herbert Austin around 1900. This was where many an Austin Seven and many a Mini had first rolled off the production lines. The Austin Seven is said to have been designed by Herbert Austin himself, in the billiard room at his home, Lickey Grange, in 1921.

In spite of the shelter of the trees, I was sweating profusely, and it was essential that I made up for the loss of fluid quickly. A chance came just before we crested the Lickey Hills, having covered about seven miles. In the days when trams were a popular means of public transport, in the first half of the century, many Birmingham families used to visit the Lickeys for a day's outing.

We were now faced with an easy four-mile descent into Bromsgrove on the B4096. As we approached the Worcestershire town, I was surprised to hear a voice call:

"Monique!"

It came from a parked car, and who should be inside, but Ken! News had been circulated from H.Q., that we should be near Bromsgrove by this time, and unlike the plan to surprise us near Wigan, which had misfired, this one had scored a bull's-eye!

Ken had very thoughtfully brought along some water, which we gladly received. Ken also relieved me of my jacket and waterproof. I was able to walk without them for the first time, since leaving John o'Groats!

Having attended to our most urgent needs, Ken then drove on, saying he would see us again on the other side of Bromsgrove.

I had been hoping to sit down to a pot of tea, somewhere on our way through the town, but I was unlucky. Perhaps such a commodity is not in great demand in Bromsgrove, at mid-day on a Saturday. We had gone right through the town, when Ken suddenly turned up again.

"I'll find somewhere where we can get something to eat," he called, and then sped off again, in his car. I'm not sure whether talking while at the driving wheel of a car was difficult, whether there was not a lot to talk about, or whether Ken was just getting his priorities right. At least, there was no time wasted on idle chatter!

The heat was beginning to sap our energy, but I knew that the stage was well within our capabilities, so I was not too concerned. About two miles along the road, a car drew up, and Ken again shouted from the open window.

"There's a Little Chef about two and a half miles up the road, I'll see you there!"

Ken rattled out the exciting news with a sense of urgency, and then roared off along the road ahead.

We now had a target to aim for, an incentive to spur us on. I looked at my watch, to estimate our time of arrival, and then maintained a fairly brisk pace - so much so, that we almost surprised Ken, when we reached the finishing-line, like two athletes racing to break the tape. I exaggerate, of course!

We had quite a long stop at the Little Chef, revived all systems, and even found time to talk. Just before we went back on the road, I succeeded in taking a photo of Ken with two of the charming Little Chefettes holding Monique, who is bedecked with my floppy sun-hat.

Ken now had to make his way home, but before

... Ken with two of the charming Little Chefettes holding Monique ...

he went, he took one last shot of us, as we went on our way, heading for Droitwich. And so we said farewell, as we slowly faded in the distance, and the sun sank rapidly in the west!

We were soon passing through Droitwich, the spa town. The name had been familiar to me in my childhood - just one of those far-away places with strange-sounding names, like Hilversum and Stuttgart, for they were all radio stations on the long wave band, which I had loved exploring on my grand-mother's wireless!

I had long since become acquainted with the real Droitwich, a quiet town set in the Worcestershire countryside, with half-timbered buildings and brine baths, popular since the Roman era. It is said that the water is effective in the treatment of rheumatism and similar complaints.

I cast a glance at some of the quainter buildings as we passed, but without holding back our advance on Worcester.

We had seven miles of flat walking to do, to reach the county town. At about 7.15, we arrived in a dehydrated state, as expected, but we had a very friendly welcome from Mrs. Horton at the City Guest House, and we were soon able to put matters right.

32. CITIES ON THE SEVERN.

It is much simpler to go through a town centre on foot, rather than by car - there are no such things as one-way streets for pedestrians, so we were almost able to make a bee-line through the heart of the city, by way of Barbourne Street, The Tything, Foregate Street and High Street.

On the way, we went through the pedestrianised shopping centre, and passed the 18th century Guildhall on the right. Next came the elaborate Gothic cathedral, which is best seen in full perspective from the county cricket ground, on the other side of the River Severn.

The next building of historical interest was the Commandery, dating from the 15th century, and headquarters of Charles II, during the battle of Worcester, in 1651. We now turned off along Bath Road, again heading into the Worcestershire countryside, and leaving behind a city of 75,000 people.

Sir Edward Elgar, composer of 'Land of Hope and Glory', was born at the nearby village of Broadheath, in 1857. It would have been precisely the right moment for his stirring music to have filled the air. If only the thrilling 'Pomp and Circumstance' marches could have pounded out the rhythm, as we strode along! Alas, there was no marching band to keep us company - except in my imagination!

It looked as though we were in for another hot day in the sun, till the sky became more hazy, and a light breeze began to blow. Having gone four miles, we came to the village of Kempsey where, at L'Aventure, both liquid refreshment and friendly encouragement were offered.

We made headway along the valley of the Severn, on the flat A38. I glanced to the right and was greeted by a fine view of the Malvern Hills in the distance, with their distinctive profile rising sharply above the plain, while to our left, were the more confused Cotswolds.

It was 11 miles to Tewkesbury, the next town on our route. We were therefore enjoying a quiet and relaxed spell of walking, passing through the village of Severn Stoke to the intersection of the A38 with the M50, the so-called Ross Spur. Meanwhile, the heat had become very unpleasant and was steadily wearing away at our reserves of energy and moisture.

Just when the need to take on more liquid was becoming very urgent, we happened to pass a fruit farm. While Monique was drinking some cool, clear water, I bought a ripe, juicy melon. When it had been cut up into segments, we went on our way. The melon provided the ideal refreshment, as we continued our journey to Tewkesbury.

Tewkesbury is a beautiful old Gloucestershire town, situated at the confluence of the Rivers Severn and Avon. It boasts a marvellous Norman Abbey, as well as many half-timbered houses and inns. We visited one of them, called curiously, The Ancient Grudge. Going along a narrow entry, at the side of the building, we came to a secluded garden, laid out with chairs and tables, complete with parasols, so that tea could be taken in the open air. What an ideal setting for taking refreshment on that warm and sunny afternoon! Monique enjoyed the restful interlude, and showing her usual bonhomie, made friends with all and sundry.

We were feeling a lot fitter when we returned to the road, ready to take on the final ten-mile stretch of the day's journey. We were aiming for the city of Gloucester, but on the way, to add a little interest and variety, we should have the pleasure of passing through three villages - Coombe Hill, Norton and Twigworth. With no serious obstacle on the road ahead, we were able to take it in our stride and, eventually, we spotted the tower of the cathedral, which was built in the Perpendicular style.

Though we were still two miles away from Gloucester, the glimpse of the tower acted as a spur, giving us a target to aim for. The finishing point of our daily stages usually came into sight as we entered the last two miles - unless, of course, geographical features prevented this.

We had no problem in finding our abode for the night, though I made one simple enquiry, just for reassurance. Directly on our route, on the approach to the city centre, we arrived at the Albert Guest House around eight o'clock.

Things seemed to be working out generally according to plan, but in the evening, I had some telephoning to do. I had to arrange our nightly accommodation for the next few days. The following night, we planned to be within a few miles of Bristol, but I had so far been unable to obtain accommodation. This problem remained unsolved, but I did manage to sort out rooms at Cross, near Axbridge, and at Taunton, for the two following stages.

Had we had more time to spend in Gloucester, there is no doubt that we should have found plenty to interest us. It is a busy city of around 110,000 people, and a port on the River Severn. Its development through the Roman and Saxon periods can be seen in the layout of the roads. The hub of the city is formed by two main arteries crossing at right-angles, the streets being called, appropriately, Northgate, Southgate, Eastgate, and Westgate Street. Gloucester has a wealth of mediaeval architecture, the most outstanding example being, of course, the cathedral. Here, the fan tracery of the cloisters is something special!

Westgate Street has a Folk Museum, in which there are half-timbered buildings of the Tudor and Jacobean periods. There are other museums by the Victorian docks. Robert Raikes, the man who founded Sunday Schools, was born in Gloucester, in 1735.

33. SPOTTED AGAIN!

As we started out through the city centre, on the morning of Monday 16th May, it was already warm and sunny. It looked as though we were in for another hot day in the sun. There was nothing we could do about it, except drink plenty and often, in a bid to stay hydrated.

We had not gone far along Southgate Street, when we came across the local radio station, Severn Sound. Having already called in on Red Rose Radio, in Preston, I decided that we could spare the time to pay a brief visit to Severn Sound, to pass on a few details about our progress up to now, and what our plans were for the days ahead. Having handed over the salient facts about our journey, we quickly returned to our task, for we should achieve nothing by lingering!

With the docks on our right, we went out of the city, along Bristol Road and through the suburb of Quedgeley. Five miles out, the road once more joined the A38, which had made a huge detour, to by-pass the centre of Gloucester, to the east. On our right was the River Severn, while on our left, was the M5.

The straightness of the road now betrayed its origin in the days of the Roman legions. We went on for a further six miles before we came to Cambridge. We had not suddenly made a flying leap across country to the old university town, of course! Our Cambridge was a quiet village, from where we caught a glimpse of the Severn, in the distance.

It was here that we enjoyed lunching al fresco, while being careful to remain in the shade.

We were now very close to Slimbridge, over to our right. Here were the headquarters of Sir Peter Scott's Wildfowl Trust, which, it is said, contains the world's largest collection of wildfowl. The wetlands, near the Severn, are the natural habitat of swans, geese, ducks, and numerous other birds.

In spite of the heat, we were making reasonable headway, and - most important - I seemed to have solved the problem of footwear.

We were passing through the village of Newport, five miles on, when a gentleman called to us, from his garden. Mr. and Mrs. Davies had seen us earlier in the day, near Gloucester, and had suspected that something unusual was afoot! They were intrigued by our venture. They also, very kindly, offered us refreshment, which we simply could not refuse!

Revived physically and spiritually, we went happily on our way, and passed through several hamlets, before coming to Alveston, another eight

... we enjoyed lunching al fresco ...

miles along the A38. According to a guide-book, there was still a Saxon church to be seen in Alveston. In stark contrast, on our right, I could see in the distance, a remarkable piece of architecture of the twentieth century - the Severn Bridge.

The bridge was opened in 1966, and carries the M4 motorway over the Severn estuary, between Aust and Chepstow. It is said that in its first twenty years, around 200 million vehicles went across! Due to the great strain put on the bridge by such a huge amount of traffic, the structure has had to be strengthened.

As our overnight stopping-point was not yet fixed, I decided that I would start looking for bed and breakfast on reaching Almondsbury, three miles beyond Alveston. In fact, we had reached Patchway, two miles past Almondsbury, before we were able to solve our problem. After about five attempts, we received a nice welcome in a friendly atmosphere, thanks to Mr. Abrahams and his team, at the Willows Guest House.

Though it was about 9.15 when we arrived, we had completed 29 miles during the day, which meant that we had to do only 23 miles for the next stage. I considered this to be a highly satisfactory state of affairs.

34. STAND AND DELIVER!

The following day, there was to be no let-up in the dry sunny spell - a temperature of 22 degrees Celsius was forecast! All we could do was to try and remain cool, calm and collected, and drink plenty. At least, we could look forward to a very interesting walk through the big city of Bristol, seaport and hive of activity for 420,000 people. In 1497, John Cabot set sail from Bristol, on his daring voyage to unknown territories across the Atlantic.

I had known Bristol in the 1940s, as a young mechanic, in the Fleet Air Arm. In particular, I had come to know the area around Temple Meads Railway Station, where I had often changed trains, but in forty years, I suppose everything would have changed. In any case, we should be taking a route through another part of the city.

Our plan was to continue along the A38, passing through the suburbs of Filton, Horfield and Bishopston, but where it made a detour, we would keep straight on, through Cotham, and along Colston Street.

The six miles into the city centre presented no problem at all, and there was plenty of refreshment available, if and when required. On the way, we passed the famous Colston Hall on our right.

We then followed the ring road along Redcliffe Way, and crossed the Floating Harbour by Redcliff Bridge. Here, we paused, took in the views and savoured the atmosphere.

Deciding to put Monique in the picture, I fastened her to some iron railings at the side of the road, asking her to pose for the camera, and then crossing to take a photo from the other side of the road. Somehow, she did not appear to think much of the idea. She was again sporting my floppy sun-hat, but as a photographic model, well ... there was still something to be desired!

As I peered through the view-finder, I fancy she muttered something beneath her breath - something along the lines of:

"I'm not all that enamoured about your photography - in fact, a lot of it is pretty r-rrruff!"

I'm certain that was the last word!

"R-rrruff!", she repeated.

No, actually, she took it all in very good part, having grown quite accustomed to my funny ways.

Once more on the move, we turned to the right and crossed the River Avon by Bedminster Bridge, to find ourselves back again on the A38. The city now receded behind us, and when we reached Bristol Airport, we were already about eight miles clear of the centre. A further mile saw us at the village of Redhill.

This was where the going began to get tough. Footpaths were almost non-existant, and since we were once more forced onto the road, we again had to suffer the inconvenience of traffic. Not only that, with the sun still beating down, it was now pretty well impossible to escape from the powerful rays, now that we had left the urban scene behind.

Several stops were called for, to replenish body fluids. There was now a great scarcity of cafés, however, whereas in the city, we had been spoilt for choice. At one point, in the absence of a tea-room, or other similar establishment, we called at a roadside grocery store, and bought a couple of juicy oranges and a bottle of milk, to help delay the threat of dehydration.

The three miles to Lower Langford were easy enough, but then came a five-mile section, which was the hilliest of the day's walking. We were crossing over the western end of the Mendip Hills, on the final stage of the day, from Lower Langford to Cross.

Here we were in cheese country again, for the famous Cheddar Gorge, with its remarkable caves was situated just three miles away.

We arrived at our destination, Manor Farm, where the A371 meets the A38, near Axbridge, at ten to eight, which was surprisingly late for the 23-mile stage. No doubt, this was to some extent due to the weather.

Mr. and Mrs. Dimmock welcomed us and made us feel at home. We were staying at an old 16th century farmhouse, which had once been a coaching inn.

Later that evening, I went out into the village and had a meal at a 17th century inn. The White Hart Hotel was located in the centre of the village of Cross, just west of the A38. The main highway for the stage-coaches passed through the village. It is said that the travellers were very relieved to arrive safely at Cross, or Axbridge, in those days when highwaymen were notoriously active! Perhaps we had arrived not a moment too soon!

35. BUCKS AND BUCCANEERS.

But for our misfortune in the Lake District, and the enforced seven days of rest, to allow Monique to recover from injury, we should, by the end of today, have reached Land's End. However, there was nothing to be gained by looking back, and thinking of what might have been. No amount of 'if-onlys' would alter a thing. The facts were that, since the start of our journey from John o'Groats, five weeks had now gone by, and there still remained seven days of walking to do. We had completed 700 miles, and Land's End was now no more than 173 miles away.

We had broken the back of the challenge, and our own backs were far from broken!

Our programme for the day was a 26-mile stage, at the end of which, we should be in Taunton, in the heart of the West Country, and deep into the land of Somerset cider. With a certain degree of confidence, we set out on the first five miles of the stage, taking us to East Brent.

Our faith in the British weather was restored, when we were greeted by a cool northerly wind, soon followed by refreshing rain. But for one day, we had just undergone eight days of hot weather! Now, at last, the heat-wave had relented.

On arriving at East Brent, we began to think about refreshment, and only a mile further on, a café unexpectedly appeared, at the left of the road, and almost on cue! Situated in the village of Brent Knoll, it was called, rather curiously, The Goat House. There could be a few thirsty, or hungry travellers unwittingly passing it by, with a name like that!

The reason for the name is quite simple, however. As well as being a café, The Goat House was also a vivarium, containing a large number of goats of various breeds. They were very friendly, and enjoyed receiving visitors, we were told. I was amused to note that, on the toilet doors, instead of the more usual terminology, the genders were shown as 'bucks' and 'does'! How confusing! Silly billies!

Brent Knoll is, in part, named after a strangely isolated knoll, or round hill, which dominates the flat wetlands for miles around. The top of the knoll, 450 feet above sea level, was once the site of an Iron Age fort.

Inspired and revived, we again headed south-westward along the A38, and at Highbridge, two miles on, we were within a mile of the seaside at Burnham-on-Sea. We were more interested, however, in exploring the town of Bridgwater, which was seven miles further on.

Bridgwater, with a population of over 30,000, was the birthplace of Admiral Robert Blake, in 1599. Blake was the successful hero of several naval engagements. As we walked through the streets of the town, filled with shoppers, we came upon his statue. This time, Monique sat proudly, at the feet of the great seafarer, while I took their photograph. There was an obvious rapport between the characters of the two models, both of them having a predilection for water. Monique was, no doubt, pretending to be an old sea-dog!

.. Admiral Robert Blake and Monique (that other well-known sea-dog) ..

Crossing the River Parrett, we left Bridgwater, on the final eleven miles to Taunton. We stayed with the A38 and, very soon, we were in the village of North Petherton. We now began to by-pass the southern end of the Quantock Hills, which were on our right. However, our road remained fairly flat, and even had footpaths, so we were able to make pretty good progress.

As we entered Taunton, we crossed the River Tone. The town derives its name from that of the river. With 49,000 people within its borders, it is the county town of Somerset. It has a pleasant location, nestling in the vale of Taunton Deane, and, among the places worth visiting, is a castle, dating from the twelfth century.

We made our way along Bridgwater Road and through the centre of the town, via East Street, Corporation Street and Park Street. We completed the stage in Wellington Road, with a nice welcome from Mrs. Evans.

It was just after half past seven, and Monique was feeling somewhat hungry. Fortunately, I was able to obtain her favourite dog-food at the garage store, just across the road. Because of the healthy, active life she was leading, Monique had a splendid appetite, and was able to manage two tins a day! Having satisfied the needs of Monique, I went back into the town to restock my own reserves of energy.

36. SOME YOU WIN, SOME YOU LOSE!

Next morning, we set off for Tiverton, which was a relatively short 20-mile spin away. It was raining - and it continued to rain during the whole journey into Wellington, six miles south-west! To feel refreshing rain on the face was fine - but you can have too much of a good thing! We were pleased, therefore, to reach Wellington, where a convenient café provided the opportunity not only to take refreshment, but also to dodge the rain. This was not strictly true for, although Monique did share my cheese sandwich and cream pastry, she still had to look in at the window with a forlorn expression.

Wellington, like Taunton, can trace its origins to Saxon times. It gave its name to the Iron Duke, and erected a monument to him. Built in the form of an obelisk, it is a prominent landmark, overlooking the town from the Blackdown Hills, two miles to the south.

By the time we were ready to leave, it had stopped raining, and the sun was breaking through. Shortly after leaving the town, we chanced to pass a roadside telephone box. I decided to take the opportunity to get in touch with an address in Tiverton, where I hoped we should be able to obtain accommodation for the night. The address was that of a farm, and was at Little Holwell, about a mile and a half south of Tiverton. I had not managed to find an address in the town, itself.

It was with some relief that I received the information from Little Holwell, that there was indeed a room available for us, that evening.

Excellent! Now, all we had to do, was get there!

Having gone a few more miles along our route, we happened to pass a transport café. This time, Monique was made more than welcome. Some of the 'gentlemen of the road' even offered her a few of their chips, which more than compensated for having to sit out in the rain, in Wellington.

The A38 twisted this way and that for about nine miles, and crossed the M5 a couple of times, on the way to Sampford Peverell. About a mile before the village, the road divided into two. A trunk-road provided an alternative route for through traffic, to the north of Sampford Peverell and Tiverton. Naturally, we took the older road, which went through the centre of the village. We were now only about five miles from Tiverton, by way of Halberton and the B3391.

We took advantage of a convenient tourist information centre, where a very helpful lady provided us with a street plan of Tiverton, and also showed us how to find our way to Little Holwell.

Such was our confidence, that we did the last few miles at a fairly brisk rate, turning left at the Town Hall, as directed. Still following our instructions, we soon crossed a small bridge and turned right. This brought us onto a rough track, running alongside the River Exe. Now and again, we met someone coming the other way, who verified that we were on the right track and heading in the right direction.

At last, we arrived at the farm where I had booked our room, and it was still only half past six. The gentleman who had spoken to me on the phone was there to meet us. He had some news - some good ... and some bad! First came the bad news - he had discovered, as soon as he had put down the phone, that the room he had offered was already booked! He had arranged for us, however, the possibility of accommodation at Halberton, and offered to take us there by car.

When I had recovered from the shock, I sized up the situation. The acceptance of alternative accommodation, in itself, was no real problem, but the accommodation which was offered, was in Halberton, four miles to the east of Tiverton, and the village through which we had passed, about an hour and a half before! Having to do these four miles again the next day, would bring that day's total to 33!

I agreed to talk to the lady who had so kindly offered the new room and reluctantly accepted the lift to Halberton. Psychologically, it was very painful, returning to Halberton - almost soul destroying! Destiny, and circumstances beyond our control, were forcing us back over miles we had already covered, with honest toil and sweat!

"Go back four squares!" were the words on the card which I had just turned over, in my imaginary board game. Unfortunately, I was hardly in the mood for playing games!

When we met Mrs. Loveday, in Halberton, I explained that staying at Halberton would mean that we should have to walk four miles which we had already walked. She immediately suggested a way to overcome the problem - Mr. Loveday had to drive into Tiverton, the next morning, and would be able to take us with him.

Splendid! I had turned over a new card, bearing the words:

"Advance four squares!" It was not such a bad game, after all!

Lake Farm, which fate had decreed would be our abode for the night, was a 17th century farmhouse, and Mr. Loveday was a sheep farmer.

That evening, I was on my way into the village for a meal, when, as I passed a field, I noticed a ewe rolling on her back and, I thought, in some distress, while a young lamb looked on helplessly, with what surely was a very pained expression. I returned to Mr. Loveday, to pass on the information.

It appears, the ewe had lost her balance on the uneven surface, and because of the weight of her heavy fleece, she was unable to get back on her feet. Mr. Loveday was soon on the scene to give her a helping hand, and in a moment, she was up on her feet again and running round, while a greatly relieved little lamb looked on!

On returning to the farmhouse after the meal, I happily turned over some pieces of music and picked out a few notes on a piano - though none too accurately, in the fading light.

The next morning, in broad daylight, I gave a better performance - though not a lot!

37. FORTIFIED.

It was time to go.

Once more, we journeyed between Halberton and Tiverton, driven this time by Mr. Loveday, and in the right direction. Mr. Loveday dropped us off in Fore Street, near the Town Hall, where, the previous evening, our pointless detour to Little Holwell had begun. After saying farewell, we braced ourselves for the day's allotted task.

We had considered the possibility of taking the A373, to Withleigh, and then turning off along country roads, heading south-west, and aiming for Copplestone. However, remembering our futile experience in Cumbria, and the fact that country roads tend to wander, like drunkards, all over the place, we played safe and chose to stay with the major roads, by way of Bickleigh.

It was half past nine, and the sun was already shining brightly, as we left Tiverton, a pleasant old market town. We crossed the River Exe, and turned immediately south, on the A396. The road stayed close to the right bank of the river and, four miles on, by-passed Bickleigh, most of which was situated on the opposite bank. On our side, we had a medieval fortified manor.

We now turned away from the valley of the Exe, to tackle the eight-mile section on the A3072 to Crediton. Along the way, we passed through the village of Stockleigh Pomeroy. We could now testify that Devon does have its ups and downs. We had quite a healthy appetite when we reached Crediton, and promptly attended to it by calling at the Crediton Inn.

When we came to leave the small market town, we turned to the west, and struck out along the A377. The afternoon sun shone at intervals, so it did not do too much damage. It was just as well, since the chance to take refreshment did not occur very often. We had to go a further eight miles, passing through Copplestone, before we managed to obtain the much needed sustenance at The Arrow, appropriately located in Bow. I suspect the landlord was a Mr. Archer. At least, he scored a bull's-eye when he brought us toasted tea-cake, apple pie and ice cream. We were fortified for the next part of our journey.

At about half past six, the sun dipped below the hedges. It meant, of course, that the temperature would also begin to drop, and encouraged me with the thought that we should now be able to make better use of our energy. We still had ten miles to do, to reach Okehampton, which was to be our resting place for the night. I had yet to find accommodation. I did have one or two addresses, however.

By-passing North Tawton on our right, we turned off the A3072, when we came to the B3215, branching off to the left. We advanced quite well over this section, and arrived in Okehampton by 9.15.

I checked my addresses, in Station Road. After one simple enquiry, we were there in no time. At the very first attempt, we managed to stay with Mr. and Mrs. Tolman. Our good fortune in finding a room so easily, helped to make up for the unhappy experience of the previous day.

This day, we had had to be on our mettle, for we had been tested by the hills of Devon. However, Monique had been equal to the task, and we had successfully completed our 29-mile schedule. This had been the last of the really long stages, so, for the first time, we began to feel that our ultimate goal, Land's End, was within our grasp!

38. A TYPICALLY ENGLISH SCENE.

Okehampton is quite a small, but attractive market town, located on the fringe of Dartmoor. In West Street, there was a museum, in which an imaginative recreation of Dartmoor life through the ages could be seen.

Before leaving the town, in the morning, we wandered along a quiet, narrow road, and were rewarded with a picturesque view of the ruins of a castle, built on a hill, in the Middle Ages.

As the road was deserted at this time, Monique was temporarily free to make her own way. She was obviously enjoying the rare, albeit brief, moment of liberty, trotting off to investigate the way ahead, turning to see if I was still following in the right direction, and then continuing the exploration. Unfortunately, this pleasant start to the day was soon brought to a close. We were about to merge with the main traffic route, the A30, so poor Monique had to go back on the lead.

We were now at the northern limits of Dartmoor National Park. High Willhays and Yes Tor, the two highest points, both over 2,000 feet, were about two miles away to our left.

Happily, we had not come across any escaped convicts! In fact, the people more likely to be making a quick getaway were the tourists!

It was Saturday, and this, no doubt, was the reason we were meeting a steady stream of holiday traffic, making an early start from all parts of Cornwall and the South-west, and hoping not to get into a jam. Since the A30 had no footpaths, we had to share the road with the motorists, a state of affairs which was far from satisfactory. We managed as well as we could, though. After all, we had dealt with the problem before.

For such a busy tourist route, the opportunity to stop for food and drink occurred very infrequently. In fact, we had gone ten miles before we were able to satisfy our thirst and hunger. At a tiny village called Lewdown, someone had thoughtfully provided a Little Chef restaurant.

We began to leave Dartmoor behind, and we now had our sights set on Launceston. According to the Cornish tourists who had transported us to the vet, in Kendal, Launceston is pronounced Lawn-s'n.

It was eight miles from Lewdown to Launceston. Having gone through the village of Lifton, and progressed to within two miles of Launceston, we reached a point where our road split into two. A by-pass carried all the through traffic to the south of the town, while the older road still led to the town centre. Naturally, we chose the pretty way, a quiet and peaceful country road, lined with hedges.

It was a pleasant change to get away from the busy trunk road, into a rural setting. We came to a small bridge, and were about to cross the River Tamar when, quite unexpectedly, my eyes were drawn to what I think can be described as a typically English scene.

In a field on our left, were fifteen men, clad in white, positively radiant in the brilliant sunshine. They were moving about at random, on the large grassy arena. Had we chanced upon the last vestige of ancient druidic ritual? On second thoughts, no – today was Saturday 21st May, and the bat, the bowler's arm and the sport of cricket, itself, were all in full swing!

This would make a good photo, I thought, as I put my floppy sun hat on Monique's head, and directed her attention to the cricket match.

"Not that sloppy fun hat, again!" she protested, and it immediately fell round her neck. I was about to correct her Spoonerism, but then, I thought: "Perhaps she is right, after all!"

She sat down and peered through a gap in the hedge to find out what the score was. I captured the moment with my camera, for the benefit of posterity.

The Tamar eventually flows out into the English Channel at Plymouth and, for much of its length, is the boundary between Cornwall and Devon.

For the first time in our lives, we were setting foot in the county of Cornwall, a fact which undoubtedly added spice to the remaining miles of our journey.

There was also the realisation that, with only two more days to go, we had to make the most of our opportunity, savour the experience, as we went along, and retain as much as possible, in memories and impressions.

We reached Launceston just before six, which was lucky, for we were just in time to obtain a pot of tea, and so stave off the possible onset of dehydration.

Our tour of the former capital of Cornwall had to be brief. Though there was a ruined Norman castle, it would have to wait for another day. We still had just over three miles of the A30 to do, before we completed our schedule for the day, which would take us to Kennards House. On our way out of Launceston, following road signs, we 'looped the loop' around the town, like a flock of pigeons, or a pilot in an aircraft, turning to find the right compass bearing, before heading out towards the west.

It was about 7.30 when Mr. and Mrs. Davey welcomed us, at Trethorne Leisure Farm. While it was still light, we had a brief stroll round the farm, to see some of the animals. Monique was particularly keen to meet the collie who worked on the farm. She also got on famously, as always, with our fellow guests.

We had a very peaceful night's sleep and, in the morning, there was no need for an alarm, or a call for breakfast. Apparently, at this time of year, a sort of ritual took place. The cows who had recently calved, paraded slowly past our window, on their way to see their offspring, for the first time in the day.

As they trooped past, they were all cheerfully exchanging news, and comparing notes, some lowing in E flat, while others bugled, in a shrill C sharp minor. With a few cow-bells thrown in, we could have had a fair backing for 'Oh, what a beautiful morning!', the song from 'Oklahoma'!

By the time the 'Carnival of the Animals' had finished parading, we were well and truly awake!

'Oh, what a beautiful morning!'

39. STONE CIRCLES AND ROUND TABLES.

Monique had made so many friends at Trethorne Leisure Farm, that we did not manage to get away until ten to ten, despite the rude awakening! The day's assignment was a 26-mile stage to Victoria. We were expecting the weather to remain dry, and the temperature to rise no higher than 17 degrees Celsius, so some pleasant walking was in prospect.

Mr. Allis, the Town Clerk of Bodmin, had been particularly helpful, when I had sought advice about the stage, which involves the crossing of Bodmin Moor. He had very kindly sent me a map, on which were marked the places where it was possible to leave the A30 and use a road without the constant streams of traffic, while still keeping a fairly straight line.

Of course, there are plenty of quiet roads. The art is to find the ones which maintain the right direction, and do not increase the overall length of the journey.

After the first mile on the A30, we were able to turn off right and go four miles along quiet country roads, passing through the villages of Polyphant and Five Lanes, to Trewint. Here, just off to the left of the road, we found the famous cottage, where the preacher, John Wesley, made several visits, in the 18th century.

We now rejoined the A30 and began our trek across the desolate, yet beautiful Bodmin Moor. In the distance to our right, one peak seemed to stand out above all the rest. This was Brown Willy, 1375 feet above sea level, and the highest point on the moor.

I had taken the precaution of carrying a few oranges, to counteract the loss of moisture. Having tethered Monique to a suitable post, I sat on top of a five-barred gate and proceeded to eat an orange. It was not a good idea! Indeed, it was tantamount to throwing caution to the wind!

The wind was blowing across the moor from the south, and the sudden gusts were so fierce, that I was nearly blown off my perch twice! Twice was enough! The third time could prove fatal! I clambered down and sat in a more secure position, on the grass.

We felt the full force of the wind later on, on the higher and more exposed parts of the moor. At least, we should be able to stay cool, in spite of the sun.

A mile and a half to our left, was a pool. Though we could not see it, it was clearly marked on a map. It was Dozmary Pool, from the water of which, a hand is said to have appeared to grasp the sword, Excalibur! Yes, we were passing through the village of Bolventor, in the kingdom of King Arthur, and the Knights of the Round Table.

Bodmin Moor stretches from Trewint to Bodmin - a distance of almost 15 miles. Almost half way across, we took a minor road, leaving the A30 and going left through a strange place called Temple. We were well away from the beaten track, now, and I could even allow Monique to run loose, at times.

The moor is a mysterious region, just waiting to be discovered. As well as its connections with Arthurian legends, there are also some huge stone circles, the exact significance of which, has puzzled humanity for centuries. Commercially, the moor is an important source of China clay, or kaolin, a fine white clay used in the manufacture of porcelain.

Perhaps we had been through a time-warp, but now, as we were coming to the edge of the moor, we again had to come to terms with civilisation in the twentieth century. It was still possible, however, to avoid much of the traffic, by taking an older road, right of the A30.

We were two miles from Bodmin, but even at that distance, there was a conspicuous landmark, a tall obelisk, which loomed ahead, beckoning us towards the centre of the town.

We eventually entered the town by way of Old Callywith Road, and so on into Castle Street. The county town of Cornwall is quite small, with around 12,000 people. On this Sunday afternoon, the streets were almost deserted.

Leaving Bodmin, we took the A389, in the direction of Lanivet. Our next road, once used by stage-coaches, went off to the right, and passed through a hamlet called Lamorick. This final section of about six miles was direct and peaceful, but decidedly hilly!

In spite of the hills, we arrived at our destination at around half past seven. The Victoria Guest House was conveniently situated, about a hundred yards off the A30, on the left. Both Monique and I were pleased with the day's adventure, and enjoyed a comfortable night in the care of Mr. and Mrs. Borer. Mrs. Borer was especially proud of her carrot cake, which, I have to confess, was rather nice!

40. LOCKED OUT!

It was the last day but one, and there was no longer any doubt that we should reach Land's End. We left Victoria, progressing steadily into a light head-wind and an occasional drizzle. The traffic on the A30 was again heavy, but, by this time, we were quite used to it!

Having gone about five miles, we passed through a village which was curiously named Indian Queens, and in the neighbouring village, Fraddon, we called at the Blue Anchor, where we took our first break, coffee with a cheese sandwich. However, our next feeding point was very elusive.

For some reason or other, we went through the four tiny villages of Summercourt, Mitchell, Carland and Zelah, without finding either food or drink! We had reached Blackwater, about 14 miles on, before we were, at last, successful. At least, it meant that we kept forging ahead, and we survived.

We now came to the final seven miles of the day's journey, and they were the most interesting and the most hospitable.

Our destination was Camborne, and at about the half-way point, came the town of Redruth. The A30 by-passed both towns, to the north. If we went through the town centres, we should only come across local traffic,

and in any case, there would be footpaths. It would also be interesting
to find out what the towns were really like.

The two towns together have about 35,000 people, and owe their rise
to the Cornish tin and copper mining industries. Redruth claims to have
been the first town in the world to have been lit by gas! Even now, its
character seemed to belong to the 'old world', and perhaps it can remain
that way.

It was here that steam railways were invented, soon after 1800. In
1771, Richard Trevithick was born near Redruth. He demonstrated his new
invention, a steam-driven carriage, in Camborne, in 1801. A year or two
later, he proved the viability of steam locomotives running on railways.

It was about eight o'clock, as we walked through Camborne. Calling
at Tyacks Hotel, we were offered excellent accommodation, which was much
appreciated. The staff, of course, made a lot of fuss over Monique, and
were very impressed by her achievement.

The following morning, I was down early for breakfast. As I needed
a film for my camera, I decided it would save time if, while I waited, I
slipped out and bought one immediately. What a shock, when I arrived at
the hotel again, about ten minutes later!

During my brief absence, someone had locked the door, and I was not
able to get in. I walked round the hotel, peering in at various windows
and trying to attract attention. The more conventional methods of entry
- knocking on the main door and ringing a bell, had been to no avail. I
eventually managed to catch someone's eye, as I looked through a window,
and managed to convince the member of staff that I really was one of the
guests, and had not yet had breakfast!

Well - I suppose it just had to happen, sooner or later!

41. THE FINAL ASSAULT.

It was Tuesday 24th May, 41 days after we started to walk from John o'Groats. We were about to begin the final assault on Land's End, now a mere 24 miles away.

During the six weeks of our journey, we had experienced the various kinds of weather. We had suffered with exhaustion in the heat-waves and we had been drenched by the occasional heavy rain. More often than not, we had met the wind head on and, of course, we had always headed more or less into the sun, when it shone. When we set off for the last time, we were met by a blustery, south-westerly wind.

On this last day, we had two towns, Hayle and Penzance, which would help to break up our journey into manageable sections. Connor Downs was soon behind us, and we arrived in Hayle, seven miles from Camborne, just when we were thinking of lunch.

Hayle is a small port, situated at the mouth of the River Hayle, on St. Ives Bay. There are some sandy beaches nearby, but we had to attend to the need for refreshment, and immediately set off again on the seven-mile section into Penzance.

It rained nearly all the time, as we crossed over from the Atlantic to the English Channel, through the villages of Canonstown, Crowlas, and Longrock. As we approached the coast, the unmistakable rocky outline of St. Michael's Mount appeared, just off the shore from Marazion. Perched on top of the granite mass, are a 14th century castle and its chapel. A causeway makes it possible to reach the rock on foot, at low tide.

On the opposite side of the Channel, just off the Breton coast, the Mont Saint Michel is remarkably similar, and has the same attraction.

The A30 now followed the sandy coastline into Penzance. On arrival at the large fishing port, population 20,000, I recalled the operetta by Gilbert and Sullivan, and wondered where the pirates were.

We climbed the main street, Market Jew Street, with its rather odd, raised pavement and, quite by chance, came upon a vegetarian restaurant, called The Olive Branch. It was now late afternoon, so we went in for a meal, to sustain us on the final section of the day. We were absolutely soaked by the rain, but we soon began to dry out. Meanwhile, it finally stopped raining!

On hearing of our exploits, fellow diners became quite excited, and Monique, as usual, received a lot of affection, which she returned, with interest. The proprietor at once got in touch with the local newspaper,

'The Cornishman', and I was asked to speak to a reporter, on the line.

Such excitement! But Land's End was still ten miles away, so there was no time to linger, if we were to arrive there before dusk.

As we approached the top of Market Jew Street, we came face to face with the stone figure of the celebrated scientist, Sir Humphry Davy, who was born in Penzance, in 1778. Among many important discoveries was the identification of several chemical elements, but he is remembered mainly as the inventor of the miner's safety lamp.

As we advanced steadily over the last ten miles, it gradually began to sink in that our great adventure was nearing its end, and I had mixed feelings. There had been times when things had not gone well - when the going had been tough. On the other hand, we were close to achieving the experience of a lifetime, so I had a tinge of regret. The challenge and the anticipation of getting up each day, beginning a fresh adventure and discovering pastures new, would be missed by both Monique and me.

The sky was still largely overcast, but at about seven o'clock, for the first time in the day, the sun made a brief appearance. Peering out from behind the dark clouds, the golden orb looked down, and saw one man and his dog heading for Land's End, with about three miles to go.

"Probably came from John o'Groats," it yawned, and then slowly drew a cloud across its face and retired for the night.

Away to our right, the silvery sea of Whitesand Bay came into view, while in the foreground, cows were grazing peacefully in a meadow.

Just before eight o'clock, we arrived at Land's End. We stood near the edge of the granite cliffs and looked down at the sea, crashing into the rocks below, more or less as it had done at John o'Groats. It would probably continue the assault, until the end of time.

Things had recently been happening at Land's End. A large area had been developed into a sort of exhibition centre, or leisure park, with a variety of buildings providing attractions for all the family. Although not finished, there were, nevertheless, several visitors wandering round the place, having a preview, perhaps.

In one building, a lady was surrounded by a brilliant exhibition of domestic lighting. In another, some workmen were having the traditional English tea-break.

We had come to the end of our journey, and I felt that we ought not to go back home without at least letting someone know of our experience. In the absence of an official to register our crossing of the finishing-line, I turned to one of the couples, walking round.

... the golden orb looked down ...

"We've just walked from John o'Groats," I said, modestly.

Now a remark like that, I think, ought to create a bit of reaction. At least, it ought to spark off some interesting conversation. Possibly I had not sounded very convincing?

"Oh, that's a long way," was the casual reply, as they continued to look at some of the buildings. Somehow, it did not have the same impact as 'Hail the conquering hero!", I thought.

We wandered round the complex of buildings and went over to look at The First and Last House. Of course, this, like almost everything else, at that hour, was closed for the night. As we turned back and crossed a field, I released Monique. She scampered round the field, as if she had been waiting long for this very moment of freedom. Wherever did she get the energy? Did she have some sort of intuition that we had come to the end of our journey? I wonder!

42. CORNWALL BY NIGHT.

One of the things I had completely overlooked, when I first planned the enterprise, was the point at which we should catch a train to return home. It had never occurred to me that B.R. might not start from Land's End, even if we managed to get there! The nearest station was, in fact, in Penzance, so I was informed, by 'the lady of the lamps'.

There were no buses at that time of night, so we slowly headed back towards Penzance. There was no rush - our mission had been accomplished and the big event was all over. We could now relax and walk at whatever speed we liked.

About a mile from Land's End, we came to the village of Sennen, for the second time within an hour. This time, I thought it prudent to call at The First and Last Inn, where we satisfied our need for refreshment.

Before we left, I wrote down the brief facts concerning our walk on a serviette, and handed it to a barmaid. In return, she gave me a beer-mat, which bore the name of the inn. If ever I find our exploit hard to believe, I can look at the beer-mat and say:

"Well, we must have done it - after all. this is the medal!"

It was almost dark when we resumed our journey. There was hardly a light shining, for miles around. When a light did appear, it was nearly always from an approaching car. We were tired, of course, but it was an unusual experience, and this gave us an extra impetus. Although we were starting and finishing at sea level, the miles in between included quite a lot of climbing, as we were only too well aware, having just travelled the road in the reverse direction.

A faint glow in the sky ahead indicated that Penzance was out there somewhere, and encouraged us to keep going. I considered that now was a good time to draw upon our emergency stock of glucose tablets. If I did not suddenly feel exceedingly energetic, they would at least give a lift to morale. As usual, I offered a few pieces to Monique, who, yet again, was revealing prodigious stamina!

It seemed a long, long time before we had a clear view of the first lights of Penzance, and it was after midnight, when we arrived. We made straight for the railway station, somewhat disappointed to find that our train was not due to leave until 5.19 a.m.

We sat down on a wooden bench, on a draughty platform, and snuggled closely together, to make the most of our body heat. During the days of the heatwave, my waterproof had drained me of moisture, but it was quite inadequate now, to keep out the chill air of early morning.

I finally decided it would be wiser to leave the station and go for a stroll round the deserted streets of the town. At least, we should be creating a little heat, instead of slowly freezing!

As we once more climbed Market Jew Street, Sir Humphry Davy gave us a stony glare, as he gazed down from his plinth. He seemed not to worry about the falling temperature, but, right now, we could have used one of his famous lamps.

We turned a corner and were stopped in our tracks, for we were face to face with one of the notorious Pirates of Penzance! Cutlass in hand, he leered down at us with blood-curdling countenance. His features were picked out clearly by the bright light, illuminating the inn-sign. Have no fear! True to Gilbert and Sullivan tradition, the Police were at the ready. On several occasions, a police car, on night patrol, had spotted us with its headlights.

Slowly, dreadfully slowly, the time passed, as we resumed our seat, on the bleak platform. At last, the train pulled into the platform, and we were able to seek the warmth of the railway carriage.

43. RETROSPECT.

Obviously, after such a long period of physical effort, and burning up of calories, we had both lost weight - in my case, about 16 pounds. That was to be expected, and the loss would be made up before very long. There was no hurry!

What did surprise me, though, was the delayed onset of fatigue.

I had assumed that I should easily slip back into my former routine and, as each day passed, feel a little less tired. In fact, fatigue did not really hit me, until three or four days after the event, but when it did strike, it struck with a sledge-hammer blow!

For three or four days, I had neither the will nor the energy to do anything! Then, just as suddenly, I was out of the doldrums, and firing on all cylinders, again.

Perhaps, by way of explanation, I was being carried on the crest of a wave, buoyed up by a sense of achievement, in the first few days after returning home. Perhaps the adrenalin was still flowing. It might just be that I was cockahoop again! At any rate, a few days went by before I realised just how tired I was.

Maybe the scenario went something like this:

Heart (to Brain). Hello, is that you Brain? You've been giving me quite a lot of work to do, these last few weeks. I can do with a break, so I'm just going to tick over quietly for a day or so. I'm sure you'll understand.

Brain. That's quite all right, Heart. We've nothing urgent on for the next day or two. You just take it easy for a while. Keep in touch!

In events like the Tour de France, which go on for several days, or even weeks, there is a gradual wearing down process, whereby the battery storing the athlete's energy is slowly drained, as the days go by. When there are repeated physical demands made upon the body, it tries to make up the loss of energy during the periods of rest. If the period allowed for recovery between one stage and the next is too short, fatigue starts to build up, and increases, the longer the event continues.

There were times when I felt I needed a longer recovery period, but it is amazing how resilient the body is, and how quickly it can adapt to new conditions.

I noticed that, during the first week of the walk, I was at my best in the morning, and became tired as the day went on. However, after the first week, I usually made a sluggish start to the day, and got into the swing of things, towards the middle of the day - unless, of course, it was one of those days!

After it was all over, I had to get the event out of my system, not just physically, but psychologically, too. Even a week after the end of the walk, I was still going on a journey of some sort or other - in the subconscious world of dreams! Walking about 25 miles a day had become a routine. Perhaps the dreams were a mental preparation for the real life experience which my body had come to expect each day. I had to readjust mentally, as well as physically.

A few weeks before leaving home for John o'Groats, I told a friend:

"When the going gets tough, and if I reach the point when I want to call the whole thing off, I shall encourage myself by saying, 'You won't be writing that book!'"

Writing this book has been one of the rewards for going all the way to Land's End - not that any reward is needed. There can be no reward greater than actually doing the walk!

Of course, once an ambition has been achieved, it loses some of its awe and glamour, in the eyes of the person achieving that ambition. The gloss has been partly removed, because 'the impossible dream' is no more a dream, no longer impossible. It is seen in a new perspective.

No matter where our spirit of adventure had taken us, we were happy to be back home again, and to meet all our friends.

"Did you have a nice holiday?", one of them asked.

I had to think carefully, before answering. Had it **been** a holiday? I had not thought of it in those terms, but if so, it was the holiday to end all holidays!

As for Monique, my constant companion, she had been a leading lady, in more ways than one. In a 'rags-to-riches' fairy-tale, the sad little orphan, abandoned as a youngster, and left to roam the streets, had been rescued. She had grown up to become a princess and, as an explorer, had walked the length of her island, revealing prodigious energy, and powers of endurance.

Thanks to the generosity of animal lovers, she was able to show her gratitude to the Birmingham Dogs' Home, for caring for her, at a time in her life, when care and affection were needed more than anything else.

What about a final thought?

Towards dusk, when the trees begin to look like houses – when the rocks begin to look like sheep – when you start repeating "The shortest point between two lines is a straight distance" – when the sparrows are circling overhead, you know it is time to seek shelter ... or sustenance ... or both!

Monique and the author would like to thank:

the various tourist boards and local authorities on their route,
Land's End Limited,
the Land's End to John o'Groats Association,
the Lord Mayor and the City of Birmingham,
the Birmingham Dogs' Home and the many generous people who support it,
the Birmingham Post and Mail,
the Wolverhampton Express and Star,
the Cornishman,
Warwickshire and Worcestershire Life,
the British Veterans' Athletic Federation,
the Midland Veterans' Athletic Club,
Birchfield Harriers,
and all who offered help, advice and encouragement.

SUMMARY OF STAGES.   PART I.

	MILES		
JOHN O'GROATS to WICK		17	the 'warm-up'
to BERRIEDALE	26	43	first blister, strap breaks
BRORA	22	65	third fine day into head wind
ARDGUY	28	93	not counting 5 miles to Corvost
DINGWALL	26	119	via Struie Hill
DRUMNADROCHIT	26	145	first heavy rain soaks maps
INVERGARRY	25	170	warm and sunny
FORT WILLIAM	23	193	rain from Spean Bridge
BALLACHULISH	17	210	cheers for the bridge-builders
BRIDGE OF ORCHY	25	235	wild Glencoe and Rannoch Moor
TARBET	29	264	we beat my previous best effort
OLD KILPATRICK	26	290	flat country, cool and hazy
HIGH BLANTYRE	20	310	through Glasgow, new heels
ABINGTON	27	337	take wrong turn, very tired
DINWOODIE MAINS	29	366	Monique's paws show wear
METAL BRIDGE	25	391	we cross the Border
HACKTHORPE	30	421	go off course, bruise toe-nail
CROOKLANDS	27	448	Monique has a cut paw!

PART II.

GARSTANG (5 + 22)	27	475	overcast and humid
WIGAN	29	504	songs at the piano
NORTHWICH	24	528	flat country, hot
NEWCASTLE, STAFFS.	23	551	another scorcher
PENKRIDGE	22	573	gently undulating, cool
EDGBASTON	24	597	home for the night
WORCESTER	25	622	the heatwave continues
GLOUCESTER	26	648	along the Severn Valley
PATCHWAY	29	677	the feet are wearing well
CROSS, AXBRIDGE	23	700	via Bristol, still hot and dry
TAUNTON	26	726	cool wind, refreshing rain
TIVERTON	20	746	rain, mix-up over booking
OKEHAMPTON	29	775	mostly sunny over Devon hills
KENNARDS HOUSE	22	797	dehydration is the problem
VICTORIA	26	823	strong cross-wind on Bodmin Moor
CAMBORNE	26	849	occasional drizzle
LAND'S END	24	873	blustery head wind, rain